LOVING

As Jesus Loves

W9-CFK-805

Sharon A. Steele

Gospel Light

AGLOW
INTERNATIONAL

Gospel Light is an evangelical Christian publisher dedicated to serving the local church. We believe God's vision for Gospel Light is to provide church leaders with biblical, user-friendly materials that will help them evangelize, disciple and minister to children, youth and families.

We hope this Gospel Light resource will help you discover biblical truth for your own life and help you minister to adults. God bless you in your work.

For a free catalog of resources from Gospel Light please contact your Christian supplier or contact us at 1-800-4-GOSPEL or at www.gospellight.com.

PUBLISHING STAFF
William T. Greig, Publisher
Dr. Elmer L. Towns, Senior Consulting Publisher
Dr. Gary S. Greig, Senior Consulting Editor
Pam Weston, Editor
Patti Pennington Virtue, Assistant Editor
Christi Goeser, Editorial Assistant
Kyle Duncan, Associate Publisher
Bayard Taylor, M.Div., Senior Editor, Theological and Biblical Issues
Kevin Parks, Cover Designer
Debi Thayer, Designer

All Scripture quotations, unless otherwise indicated, are taken from the *Holy Bible, New International Version®. NIV®.* Copyright © 1973, 1987, 1984 by International Bible Society. Used by permission of Zondervan Publishing House. All rights reserved.

Other versions used are:
KJV—King James Version. Authorized King James Version.
MLB—Modern Language Bible, The New Berkeley Version. Copyright © 1945, 1959, 1969, 1971, 1987, Hendrickson Publishers, Inc. Peabody, MA 01960. Used by permission.
NASB—Scripture taken from the *New American Standard Bible,* © 1960, 1962, 1963, 1968, 1971, 1972, 1975, 1977 by the Lockman Foundation. Used by permission.
NEB—From *The New English Bible.* ©The Delegates of Oxford University Press and the Syndics of the Cambridge University Press 1961, 1970, 1989. Reprinted by permission.
NKJV—From the *New King James Version.* Copyright © 1979, 1980, 1982 by Thomas Nelson, Inc. Publishers. Used by permission. All rights reserved.
RSV—From the *Revised Standard Version* of the Bible, copyright 1946, 1952, and 1971 by the Division of Christian Education of the National Council of the Churches of Christ in the USA. Used by permission.

Aglow International is an interdenominational organization of Christian women. Our mission is to lead women to Jesus Christ and provide opportunity for Christian women to grow in their faith and minister to others.

Our publications are used to help women find a personal relationship with Jesus Christ, to enhance growth in their Christian experience, and to help them recognize their roles and relationships according to Scripture.

For more information about our organization, please write to Aglow International, P.O. Box 1749, Edmonds, WA 98020-1749, U.S.A., or call (425) 775-7282. For ordering or information about the Aglow studies, call (800) 793-8126.

CONTENTS

FOREWORD

When the apostle Paul poured out his heart in letters to the young churches in Asia, he was responding to his apostolic call to shepherd those tender flocks. They needed encouragement in their new lives in Jesus. They needed solid doctrine. They needed truth from someone who had an intimate relationship with God and with them.

Did Paul know as he was writing that these simple letters would form the bulk of the New Testament? We can be confident that the Holy Spirit did! How like God to use Paul's relationship with these churches to cement His plan and purpose in their lives and, generations later, in ours.

We in Aglow can relate to Paul's desire to bond those young churches together in the faith. After 1967, when Aglow fellowships began bubbling up across the United States and in other countries, they needed encouragement. They needed to know the fullness of who they were in Christ. They needed relationship. Like Paul, our desire to reach out and nurture from faraway birthed a series of Bible studies that have fed thousands since 1973 when our first study, *Genesis*, was published. Our studies share heart-to-heart, giving Christians new insights about themselves and their relationships with and in God.

God's generous nature has recently provided us a rewarding new relationship with Gospel Light Publications. Together we are publishing our Aglow classics, as well as a selection of exciting new studies. Gospel Light began as a publishing ministry much in the same way Aglow began publishing Bible studies. Henrietta Mears, one of its visionary founders, formed Gospel Light in response to requests from churches across America for the Sunday School materials she had written for the First Presbyterian Church in Hollywood, California. Gospel Light remains a strong ministry-minded witness for the gospel around the world.

Our hearts' desire is that these studies will continue to kindle the minds of women and men, touch their hearts and refresh spirits with the light and life a loving Savior abundantly supplies.

This study, *Loving as Jesus Loves* by Sharon Steele, will guide you through accepting Jesus' love and learning to extend His love to those people in your life who aren't always easy to love. I know its contents will richly reward you.

Jane Hansen

President, Aglow International

INTRODUCTION

"A new command I give you: Love one another. As I have loved you, so you must love one another. By this all men will know that you are my disciples, if you love one another." John 13:34,35

Although Jesus has commanded us to love one another, it seems that into everyone's life God sends people who are difficult to love. In addition, we all know people for whom we may have genuine feelings of love, but at times our actions toward them are filled with anger, frustration and impatience. Feelings of love seem to disappear, and we find ourselves battling feelings of disgust, disappointment or even hatred.

God wants His children to become effective, powerful Christians by learning to love with Jesus' love. Often as we attempt to love those who are difficult to love, we find ourselves locked into a fierce battle with Satan. Knowing how difficult it is to love those who have hurt us or the people we care about, Satan tempts us to be filled with unresolved anger, bitterness and hatred. He knows as we give in to those natural inclinations, we become ineffective and powerless as children of God.

Fortunately, with God's help we can learn to love others with Jesus' love. Even when we do not have feelings of love, we can choose to perform the actions of love.

The purpose of this study is threefold; through the careful examination of Jesus' love and His teachings regarding love…

1. *We can gain a clearer understanding of the true nature of genuine love.* Too often the nature of love is misunderstood, and this study will clarify what is and is not love.
2. *We will be encouraged to fully accept the love of Jesus for ourselves.* We cannot genuinely love others until the love of Jesus is active and real in our own lives.

3. *We will learn how to love even when we don't feel love for others.* You will be encouraged to put the practical actions of love into practice. We do not need to wait for feelings of love before we can perform loving actions.

As you understand, accept and practice Jesus' love, you will give the feelings of love an atmosphere in which they can grow and mature. As His love is demonstrated in you, your joy will increase and others will recognize that you are truly His disciple.

AN OVERVIEW OF THE STUDY

This Bible study is divided into four sections:

- A CLOSER LOOK AT THE PROBLEM defines the problem and helps you understand the goal of the study.
- A CLOSER LOOK AT GOD'S TRUTH gets you into God's Word. What does God have to say about what you are facing? How can you begin to apply His Word as you work through each lesson?
- A CLOSER LOOK AT MY OWN HEART will help you clarify and further apply truth. It will also give guidance as you work toward loving others with the same love Jesus has shown you.
- ACTION STEPS I CAN TAKE TODAY is designed to help you focus on immediate steps of action.

YOU WILL NEED

- A Bible.
- A notebook in which to journal additional thoughts or feelings that come up as you go through the lessons and do the action steps as directed.
- Time to meditate on what you're learning. Give the Holy Spirit time to personalize His words for your heart so that you can know what your response should be to the knowledge you are gaining.

HOW TO START AND LEAD A SMALL GROUP

One key to starting and leading a small group is to ask yourself, *What would Jesus do and how would He do it?* Jesus began His earthly ministry with a small group called the disciples, and the fact of His presence made wherever He was a safe place to be. Think of a small group as a safe place. It is a place that reflects God's heart, God's hands. The way in which Jesus lived and worked with His disciples is a basic small-group model from which we are able to draw both direction and nurture.

Paul has exhorted us to "walk in love, as Christ also has loved us and given Himself for us" (Ephesians 5:2, *NKJV*). We, as His earthly reflections, are privileged to walk in His footsteps, to help bind up the brokenhearted as He did or simply to listen with a compassionate heart. Whether you use this book as a Bible study or as a focus point for a support group, a church or home group, walking in love means that we "bear one another's burdens" (Galatians 6:2, *NKJV*). The loving atmosphere provided by a small group can nourish, sustain and lift us up as nothing else does.

Jesus walked in love and spoke from an honest heart. In His endless well of compassion He never misplaced truth. Rather, He surrounded it with mercy. Those who left His presence felt good about themselves because Jesus used truth to point them in the right direction for their lives. When He spoke about the sinful woman who washed Jesus' feet with her tears and wiped them with her hair, He did not deny her sin. He said, "her sins, which are many, are forgiven, for she loved much" (Luke 7:47, *NKJV*). That's honesty without condemnation.

Jesus was a model of servant leadership. "Whoever desires to become great among you shall be your servant. And whoever of you desires to be first shall be slave of all" (Mark 10:43,44, *NKJV*). One of the key skills a group leader possesses is the ability to be an encourager of the group's members to grow spiritually. Keeping in personal contact with each member of the group, especially if one is absent, tells each one that he/she is important to the group. Other skills an effective group leader will develop are being a good listener, guiding the discussion and guiding the group to deal with any conflicts that arise within it.

Whether you're a veteran or brand new to small-group leadership, virtually every group you lead will be different in personality and dynamic. The constant is the presence of Jesus Christ, and when He is at the group's center, everything else can come together.

YOU'RE INVITED!

To grow...

To develop and reach maturity; thrive; to spring up; come into existence from a source;

with a group

An assemblage of persons gathered or located together; a number of individuals considered together because of similarities;

To explore...

To investigate systematically; examine; search into or range over for the purpose of discovery;

new topics

Subjects of discussion or conversation.

Meeting on

Date _____ Time _____

Located at

Place _____

_____

Contact _____

Phone _____

Note: Feel free to fill in and photocopy this as an invitation to hand out or post on your church bulletin board.

One

LOVE'S TREMENDOUS IMPORTANCE

Janet attended church every Sunday and faithfully brought her tithes and offerings. She was a gifted musician whose singing had blessed many people. She was an articulate teacher who had a tremendous grasp of God's Word. Regrettably, Janet also had a quick temper and a sharp tongue that could cut a person to shreds in seconds. Although Janet had so much to offer, the lack of love in her actions negated the positive effect of her ministry. Whether Janet didn't recognize the importance of love or just didn't know how to love, her effectiveness for God's kingdom suffered dreadfully.

A Closer Look at the Problem

Loving is not always easy. We all know people who are difficult to love. Loving actions take time, energy and sometimes money, but in God's sight nothing is more important.

This first chapter will focus upon the tremendous importance of expressing God's love. Should you begin to feel discouraged by your own lack of love, don't be tempted to give up. Later chapters will give practical ways to build love into your own nature. Loving others is God's will for you and He will give you the strength you need.

As you begin this study, ask God to open your eyes to the importance of love and to speak to you through His Word. Ask Him to give you the willingness to apply the truths discovered so that you may grow in your love for others.

A Closer Look at God's Truth

1. What question did the expert in the law ask Jesus in Matthew 22:34-40?

   What was Jesus' answer?

   Why do you think Jesus gave two commands instead of one when the Pharisee had asked for the single most important commandment?

Jesus quoted both of these commands (see Deuteronomy 6:5 and Leviticus 19:18) because both are of vital importance and are related. If we love God, we will honor and obey Him, and He greatly increases our ability to love others. If we do not love others, it creates a barrier between God and us.

   How does Jesus relate these two commandments to the law and the prophets?

   What does verse 40 mean to you?

2. According to Romans 13:8-10, what debt do we always owe to others?

   What does verse 8 say about the person who loves others?

How does obeying the commandment to love fulfill the Law?

If loving is the fulfillment of the Law, what is implied when we do not love?

When we love God with all our hearts, souls and minds, pleasing Him becomes our priority. As we seek to honor Him through our lives, He increases our desire and our capacity to love others. Love for our neighbors will result in beneficial actions toward them, which means we would never seek to hurt them. Because love is clearly God's commandment to us, the person who is content to live with hatred needs to recognize that he or she is not walking in obedience to God's will.

3.   What question did the expert in the law ask Jesus in Luke 10:25-28?

How did Jesus answer him?

Why do you think Jesus answered with a question?

How are we to love God?

Describe what it means to you to love God with all your heart, soul, strength and mind.

The word *heart* refers to the center of one's emotions, even as we today would say someone "broke my heart." *Soul* refers to the inner self or personality and *strength* is a reference to one's physical body. The word *mind* refers to the intellect. By putting them together, the commandment implies loving God with one's entire being.

How did He say we are to love others?

What does loving your neighbor as yourself involve?

What was Jesus' response to the expert's answer (v. 28)?

How does loving God relate to salvation and trusting in God?

How does loving others relate to your salvation?

Jesus emphasized that loving God is the most important commandment. It is vital to our salvation. Unless we love God, we can't expect to gain eternal life and unless we first love and accept Him, we can't love others with His kind of love. Loving God enables us to trust Him and to submit to His lordship. As we love Him and accept His lordship over us, He increases our ability to love others.

Take a few minutes to evaluate the depth of your love for God. In what ways does your love need to grow?

4. According to Luke 10:29-37, what other question did the expert ask and what do you think was his motive for asking (v. 29)?

How did Jesus answer his question?

Why do you think Jesus answered with a parable, and what did He accomplish with His answer?

In the parable, why do you think the priest and the Levite went by without stopping? What did their lack of action show?

How do their reasons compare to reasons why people today fail to help others?

What practical demonstrations of love did the Samaritan show?

How did the Samaritan show that he loved his neighbor as himself and what did it cost him to help?

Why do you think he helped and what did he gain by helping?

How does this story define a neighbor?

In this story the neighbor was not a person who lived next door. He was not a friend or even an acquaintance. Instead, he was a person in need. The Samaritan proved his love by giving his time, effort and money to help meet that man's need. While we may not often come upon an individual who is physically wounded and bleeding, there are many who are emotionally wounded and bleeding. They desperately need someone to care and it often takes time and energy to minister to those hurting individuals. It is sad that we are often too busy or too unconcerned to get involved in the lives of those wounded souls in need of someone who cares. Helping others is love in action. Are you willing to give of yourself to reach out to those who are in need? If this is a struggle for you, ask God to give you a willing heart.

5. What gifts of the Holy Spirit are mentioned in 1 Corinthians 13:1-3?

What is the result when a person has these spiritual gifts, but lacks love?

Why are these gifts so ineffective if not accompanied by love?

Why do you think so many people seek certain spiritual gifts, rather than trying to build love into their lives?

Although spiritual gifts are desirable, we need to realize that unless they are accompanied by love, their value to us and to Christ's Body will be greatly diminished. Without love, the most impressive manifestation of gifts and the most noble sacrifices mean nothing. We must learn to love or these gifts will accomplish little. To be powerful and effective to the kingdom of God, the gifts of the Spirit must be combined with the active love of Jesus in our lives. People usually do not care how much you know until they know how much you care.

6. What does 1 John 2:9-11 tell us about the person who hates?

What do these verses tell about the person who loves?

What is promised to the one who loves?

What do you think is meant by the *darkness* and the *light*?

Verse 10 is a key to victorious living. Why do you think love is important if we are to live a victorious life in Christ?

What does verse 10 imply about hatred in our lives?

In Scripture *darkness* usually refers to any area that is under Satan's control. *Light* refers to an area controlled by God. Love is a characteristic of the light and cannot coexist with the darkness. We need to recognize that if we have an area of hatred in our lives, Satan has control of us in that area. This hatred will become a stumbling block, and we won't be able to live victoriously until we allow God to remove it.

A Closer Look at My Own Heart

Loving kind, lovable people usually presents no challenge to our ability to love. But how do you love that irritable grouch who consistently rubs you the wrong way? How do you love the one who has taken advantage of you or who has deeply hurt you or a loved one?

When you think of those who are difficult to love, does a specific individual come to mind? As you study the remaining passages, ask God to reveal practical love actions you can take to begin to build love into those more difficult relationships.

7.   According to Luke 6:27-31, who does Jesus command us to love in verse 27?

What actions of love does Jesus ask us to perform in verses 27 and 28?

How do you think obeying these commands would affect your feelings?

What effect might it have on the other individual?

What practical action of love is found in Luke 6:31?

Ask God to show you practical ways to apply verse 31 to your relationships.

8. What actions of love are commanded in Romans 12:17-21?

How do these instructions relate to the actions in Luke 6?

What is the main emphasis of these two passages?

As the apostle Paul wrote these instructions, he realized that it may be impossible to live in peace with some people. No matter how hard you try, you cannot force another individual to be at peace with you. Our task is to carefully examine our own actions to honestly determine what we can do to bring peace into the relationship. As we choose to do everything we can to promote peace and to perform the actions of love described in these verses, most people will respond favorably.

9. In Luke 6:32-36, what actions did Jesus describe that even sinners do?

In what way are Christians to be different?

What will be the results of following Jesus' instructions?

What do these verses show us about God's love?

The principles found in these passages from Luke and Romans are among the most powerful in Scripture in teaching us how to love those who are difficult to love. These scriptures are not intended to teach us to become doormats for other people. Instead they teach us the principle of overcoming evil by doing good.

A story is told of a young soldier who, because of his strong Christian beliefs, was teased unmercifully by those in his barracks. Yet every night the young man knelt by his bed to pray. One night, an especially tough sergeant picked up his dirty boots and threw them at the young praying soldier, hitting him in the head. Everyone laughed, but the young man continued to pray. The next morning the sergeant found his boots, cleaned and shined beside his bed. He was so touched by the soldier's reaction that it broke through his tough shell and he gave his life to the Lord that day. The soldier had done what he could to promote peace.

Satan wants us full of anger and bitterness. When others mistreat us or our loved ones, it is natural to want to retaliate, but retaliation increases the feelings of animosity. However, if we will choose to do good to those who hurt us, blessing and praying for them, the feelings of anger and hatred begin to dissipate. Love is one of God's most powerful weapons against the forces of Satan.

We can't always control our thoughts and feelings, but we can, by an act of the will, choose to respond to those feelings with God's love. If we will choose to pray every time we have a bitter or hateful thought toward another person, those feelings will lose their power to control us. We need to ask God to show us any actions of love that we can perform to help meet that person's need. If we do what He tells us, we will be amazed at the change in feelings. God will be honored and glorified as we show His kind of love.

Action Steps I Can Take Today

10. **Evaluate the depth of your love for God.** In your journal, honestly describe your love relationship with God. Ask God to reveal to you any areas where you are loving Him with halfhearted devotion. Then write a prayer asking Him for strength to make any needed changes.

11. **Honestly evaluate the depth of your love toward others.** Ask yourself the following:

    * Am I too busy or too unconcerned to help those in need?
    * To whom can I show God's love in a tangible way today?
    * Is a lack of love hindering my effectiveness as a Christian?

- Is hatred for anyone destroying my walk with God? (If yes, will you confess that hatred as sin and ask God to help you get rid of it?)

12. **Choose actions of love.**

- Ask God to show you those people whom you need to learn to love. Write a prayer in your journal asking God to teach you how to love with His love.
- Ask God for specific ways to pray for those who need your love. Record the ways you've prayed, so you will not forget them.
- Ask God for creative ways to demonstrate love. Make a list in your journal of all the ideas that He brings to your mind. Determine that, with God's help, you will begin to put these actions into practice. Record any actions taken and the results of your actions.

- Two -

LOVE'S INCREDIBLE POWER AND ULTIMATE SOURCE

Mary walked into the church not knowing what to expect. A close friend had invited her and she had, somewhat reluctantly, agreed to go. Throughout the worship service, she kept sensing that there was something wonderfully different about these people. They were so warm and seemed to genuinely care about each other. As the service came to a close, Mary felt overwhelmed with emotion and began to cry. When her friend asked her what was wrong, she replied, "I want what they have."

Mary had been so touched by God's love flowing through His people, that she accepted Jesus as her Savior that very night. Love's incredible power had drawn her to Him who is the ultimate source of love.

A Closer Look at the Problem

It is easy to see that God has commanded us to love and that our love or lack of love for others can be a reflection of our relationship with God. Unfortunately, just knowing those things does not necessarily make us more loving. Sometimes it is extremely difficult to love another person, and our lack of love can leave us with staggering feelings of guilt and failure. We need more than just to know we *should* love. We need an unfailing source of love who can enable us to love when our human ability to love is not enough. The dual focus of this chapter is to...

1. Realize and appreciate the incredible power of love.
2. Learn to connect to God, our ultimate source of love, and His power will enable you to love when you simply cannot love through your own strength.

Before you open God's Word, ask Him to speak to you personally and to help you apply what you learn to your life and your relationships.

A Closer Look at God's Truth

LOVE'S AWESOME POWER

1. According to Colossians 2:2,3, what was Paul's twofold intention for ministry to these people (v. 2a)?

What did he hope the result of the encouragement and unity would be (vv. 2b,3)?

2. What result of love is found in Colossians 3:14?

What role do you think love plays in uniting people and why?

Love is God's most powerful force for unifying His people. His love enables us to accept others, including their faults. This unconditional acceptance is essential to unity.

3. What result of love is mentioned in John 13:34,35?

    Why do you think this result occurs?

    What is the result in the world when Christians don't show love for each other?

Without Jesus' love, none of us has the capacity to love the unlovable or to love those who have hurt us. When we reach out in love to hard-to-love people, the world will recognize that we are different. This difference will identify us as belonging to Jesus because we are following His example of love.

4. In John 17:20-23, which phrase indicates that you are included in Jesus' prayer?

    List all the phrases from Jesus' prayer that suggest Christians are to be united and loving toward each other.

    What are the results of loving unity between Christians?

    Why does love for each other have such an impact upon unbelievers?

Love is one of God's most powerful magnets to draw us to Himself. People everywhere desperately want and need to love and to be loved. When people of the world see Jesus' love and acceptance among believers, they will be drawn to Him. Our love for each other is proof to the world that Jesus came and that He loves *all* of us. Trying to shame or condemn people into a right relationship with God usually drives them further away. Honest, caring love, as demonstrated through the life of Jesus, is God's power to draw people to Himself.

Do you know an unbeliever or a defeated Christian that you can, through love, help bring into a right relationship with the Lord? Ask God for practical and creative ways to show and express love toward that person.

5. What tragic result of division is described in Luke 11:17?

    How does this apply to a home?

    To a fellowship?

Love has the power to unite and it is only through love that a home or a church body can be built up and strengthened. Fighting, bickering and a lack of love shows that God's Spirit is not in control.

6. From 1 John 3:16-20; 4:17,18, list all phrases that suggest results of loving one another.

    What do you think is meant by 1 John 3:17? See James 2:14-17 also.

    How do our words express love?

    Why do you think actions of love will set our hearts at rest in God's presence?

    How can love drive out fear?

It is important to realize that words of love are not being condemned in these verses. Often people need to hear our expressions of love. There are times, however, when words alone are not enough. When a person has a physical, spiritual or emotional need that we can help meet, true love will express itself by helping to answer that need.

When we perform actions of love, one result is a sense of assurance that we belong to God. Sometimes our hearts condemn us and make us feel guilty even when God hasn't condemned us. Revelation 12:10 tells us that Satan is the accuser of Christians and he delights in a guilt-ridden, defeated child of God. One way in which we can receive peace and assurance of salvation is through actions of love toward others.

7. What is promised in 1 John 3:21-24?

What commands must we obey to receive these promises?

How does love or lack of love affect one's prayer life?

How do obedience and faith affect one's prayers?

Love is a condition to having prayers answered (see 1 John 3:21-23). We must believe in Jesus and we must love one another. If we have love in our hearts for others, we are much more likely to feel confident in approaching God. If we're experiencing hatred, it is extremely difficult to draw into God's presence. Faith and obedience are also important. Without faith, we limit God's power in our lives (see Matthew 13:58). If we are deliberately disobedient, we feel ashamed to draw into His presence and our prayer life is severely hindered.

8. Take a few minutes to reflect on your own prayer life. In your journal, describe how these verses apply to you and to your prayer life. List any changes you need to make before you can have power in prayer. Write a prayer asking God to help you make those changes.

LOVE'S ULTIMATE SOURCE

Annette recognized the importance of love and knew she *should* love. Unfortunately, she also knew her own heart and felt overwhelmed by the ugliness of her feelings. Unresolved anger, bitterness, hatred and doubt left her with such staggering feelings of guilt and failure that she hesitated to draw into God's presence. Why would God care about or bother to answer such a pathetic failure?

Annette had fallen prey to one of Satan's cleverest deceptions. She felt too ashamed to go to God, yet He was the *only One* able to clean her up and enable her to love. A mature Christian friend prayed with Annette that she would recognize how precious she was to God and He powerfully answered that prayer. Annette learned to walk in God's grace. As she experienced a new awareness of God's love toward her, Annette was able to draw into His presence and receive His power to love.

As you look at the following passages, ask God to show you how you can more fully connect with Him to receive His power to love.

9. According to 1 John 4:7,8,16, who is the source of love?

How is God described in verses 8 and 16?

In these verses, the Greek words that are translated as "love" are either *agape* (noun form) or *agapeo* (verb form). Both describe a benevolent, self-giving love that always seeks the highest good for the other individual. This is the way God loves us and how He wants us to love others.

What does verse 7 tell us about the person who "has been born of God"?

Describe what you think it means to be born of God.

It is important to realize that God's very nature is self-giving love and that He is the ultimate source of love. When an individual receives Jesus as Savior and Lord, that person is born of God's Spirit and God's love becomes active within the individual. As we accept Him, His Spirit indwells us and begins the renewing process. It is His Spirit within us that empowers us to love others and gives us a desire to reach out to them.

10.   Read Galatians 5:13-26. What instruction about love is given in verse 13?

What does verse 14 teach about love?

What actions are we warned against in verse 15 and why?

Describe what you think "biting and devouring each other" means.

Summarize the struggle between the sinful nature and the spiritual nature (vv. 17-26).

How can we overcome the downward pull of the sinful nature?

Describe what you think is meant by the phrase "live by the Spirit" (vv. 16,25).

List the acts of the sinful nature (vv. 19-21). Which ones show a lack of love?

List the fruit of the Spirit found in Galatians 5:22,23.

It is important to recognize that the sinful nature is always present in our lives and that it is in conflict with the spiritual nature. It is a natural tendency of the flesh to respond to hurtful situations with hatred, discord and fits of rage. Without the power of God's Spirit, we cannot respond with love. In our own strength, we cannot overcome these natural tendencies toward sin. It is only when we live by the power of God's Spirit that we are able to gain victory over them.

A Closer Look at My Own Heart

Take a few moments to consider your own heart condition, asking God to show you any of the acts of the sinful nature that may be present in your life. Confess them as sin and ask God to cleanse you.

Remember that the key to overcoming the acts of the sinful nature is to live by God's Spirit. As we do, His love within us begins to produce the fruit of the Spirit to replace the acts of the sinful nature. As we draw closer and closer to Him, the fruit of the Spirit will become more and more evident in our own lives.

11. As you read John 15:1-12, list all phrases that show the futility of trying to bear spiritual fruit through human strength and effort.

Describe what you think it means to "remain," or abide, in Jesus.

What is promised to the one who remains or abides in Jesus?

What are the results of not remaining in Jesus (vv. 4-6)?

What is the individual's responsibility?

How does this passage relate to the fruit of the Spirit?

It is essential that we recognize that God is the ultimate source of love and that love is a fruit of God's Holy Spirit. It is only through remaining closely connected to Jesus that we are able to bear the fruit of God's Spirit. When His Spirit fills and controls our lives, the natural result is love toward others and a growth of the fruit of the Spirit.

Although God is the One who produces the fruit of the Spirit, there is also an element of human responsibility. We cannot expect to grow in the Spirit unless we are intimately connected to God. We must also feed the spiritual nature through frequent worship, prayer and Bible study. Neither can we expect to grow if we are in willful disobedience to God. Remaining or abiding in Jesus implies a day-to-day, minute-by-minute relationship with Him. Without that close relationship, the fruit of the Spirit will not be produced in our lives.

12.   What result of the Spirit-filled life is found in Romans 5:5?

13.   How do the truths in 2 Corinthians 3:17,18 relate to our ability to love?

14.   Summarize what each of the following verses says about living a victorious, fruitful life in the Spirit:

Matthew 26:41

Ephesians 3:16-21

1 Peter 2:2

From the above verses, what is an area of growth needed in your spiritual life?

Which promise is most meaningful to you?

What condition is given as a requirement for fulfilling that promise?

Do you need to make any changes to be able to claim that promise? If yes, write down what changes you need to make and ask God's help in making those changes.

Through God's Holy Spirit, we have His power available to enable us to live fruitful, effective lives filled with His kind of love. Attempting to love on our own strength will only lead to frustration and failure. We must lay hold of God's power by being continuously filled with His Spirit. It is only by the power of God's Spirit that the fruit of the Spirit can be reproduced in our lives.

Many people experience a dramatic filling of the Holy Spirit. Following that experience, they see much evidence of the fruit of the Spirit in their lives. Tragically, many expect that one experience to carry them on a spiritual high indefinitely. They don't feed the spiritual nature and make no effort to grow in the Spirit. The result is spiritual disaster. They are weak and ineffective; they have no joy in the Lord and no victory. They live as defeated Christians. Unfortunately, they often bring dishonor to the name of Jesus and to the reputation of the Holy Spirit.

We cannot expect a one-time experience to empower us for life. Ephesians 5:18 commands us to be filled with the Spirit. The Greek word that is used for "filled" is in the continuous present tense which implies that we are to be filled with God's Spirit *now* and we are to *continuously* be filled. We need to seek God daily and to ask for His continuous filling and empowering. It is only as we draw near to God and let His Spirit continually fill and control us that we are able to love those who are difficult to love. If it is your desire to grow in your ability to love, strengthen your relationship with God. Keep on being filled with the Spirit.

Action Steps I Can Take Today

15. **Evaluate the power of love in your own life.** In your journal, write an honest assessment of how God's love in you is affecting others. Ask God to show you areas where you need to improve; then write a prayer asking Him for His strength to improve in those areas.

16. **Evaluate your life in regard to the acts of the sinful nature** (see Galatians 5:19-21). Review the acts of the sinful nature, asking God to reveal areas where the sinful nature may be in control of your life.

17. **Evaluate your life in regard to the fruit of the Spirit.** Review the fruit of the Spirit and identify which fruit of the Spirit is most evident in your life (see Galatians 5:22,23). Which is least evident? Ask God to show you practical ways in which you can remain more closely connected to the life-changing power of His Spirit. Write in your journal any ideas that come to mind.

18. **Choose steps to strengthen your walk with God.**

    - Ask God to show you any areas of disobedience that are hindering the work of God's Spirit in your life. In your journal write down any areas God reveals.
    - As God reveals areas of disobedience, choose to confess those as sin and turn away from them.
    - Ask God to fill you with His Holy Spirit today and in faith believe that He will. Seek the continuous filling of His Spirit.
    - Make time spent with God a priority in your life. List steps that you need to take to do this.
    - If you are struggling in loving another individual, ask God to empower you to love that person through His Spirit in you.

– Three –

LOVE IS ACCEPTING

Susan was young when she married, but was careful to marry a believer. Her mother, who was married to an unbeliever, had often told her, "If you marry a Christian, you won't have the problems that your dad and I have had." Susan married, fully expecting to have *no* problems. She knew that her new husband would always be gentle and unselfish, eager to please her and would instinctively understand and meet her emotional needs. He would be a wise, wonderful husband and father and together they would most certainly live "happily ever after."

Unfortunately, her husband had faults and didn't seem to have the vaguest idea of how to meet her emotional needs. What Susan did not realize was that no man could have lived up to her expectations. His faults and her unmet needs became her focus. Sabotaged by unrealistic expectations and a focus on the negative, the love Susan had once felt disappeared. In place of love, Susan now harbored a critical spirit and experienced great disappointment. As she struggled in the relationship with her husband, she found it more and more difficult to draw close to God. Ashamed of her feelings, she doubted that God could still love and accept her.

A Closer Look at the Problem

No human being is perfect. We all have faults. A wise person recently remarked, "You won't have a perfect marriage because you're married to a sinner. And what makes it even worse is that your spouse is married to one, too!" Often we come into relationships with unrealistic expectations. People disappoint us and fail to live up to our standards. How can we love them in spite of unmet needs and disappointments?

Beginning with this lesson, each of the remaining chapters will examine specific actions of Jesus' love toward us. We will see how we can build these same actions of love into our lives whether we have *feelings* of love or not. This chapter will demonstrate that acceptance is both an action and an attribute of love. The dual focus of this lesson is to…

1. Recognize how the love of Jesus reaches out to accept us, even with our faults and weaknesses. You will be encouraged to fully receive His accepting love for you.
2. Learn practical ways to overcome a negative focus and build accepting love into our relationships.

Before you begin the study of God's Word, ask Him to open your eyes to receive His truth and to give you a willing heart to apply what you learn.

A Closer Look at God's Truth

1. In John 13:34,35, how did Jesus command His disciples to love?

What would be the result of that kind of love?

Why do you think Jesus called this a *new* commandment, since Leviticus 19:18 also commands us to "love your neighbor as yourself"?

One step up- Love as Jesus loves.

Although the Old Testament does command us to love our neighbor, these verses from John 13 present a new standard of love. We are now given the command to love others "as Jesus loved us." This is definitely a newer, higher standard of love.

What words or phrases would you use to describe the love of Jesus?

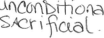

unconditional   accepting
sacrificial.   forgiving

THE ACCEPTING LOVE OF JESUS

2. According to Romans 5:8, how is the love of God demonstrated?

What phrase implies that Jesus' love is accepting?

3. What do the following verses tell about God's love and acceptance?

John 3:16,17

1 John 3:1 — *child of God*
we are family

4. How is God described in Ephesians 2:4-9?
Rich in mercy
kind

What does God's love do for us?

5. According to Luke 15:11-24, what were the actions of the younger son that would make it difficult to accept him?

Why did he decide to return to his father?

What emotions do you think the son felt as he drew close to home?

How do you think he felt as he saw his father running toward him?

How did the father demonstrate his loving acceptance of his son even before the son asked for forgiveness? How did the father show that he accepted him *as a son*?

6. In Luke 15:25-32, how did the older brother react to his brother's return?

father is demonstrating grace – Older brother is working

What was his focus? *his way to grace.*

What do you think would have happened to the younger brother if the father had acted the way the older brother did?

What effect did the older brother's lack of acceptance have upon the father? *Father was resolute. – Did not change his celebration of his son returned.*

How was the older brother's attitude affected by his unwillingness to accept his brother? *Showed his jealousy –*

symbolic – rejoice with the father when one brother is found.

36

What does this parable show about the love of God?

The accepting and forgiving love of God is beautifully portrayed in this parable. The younger son had made a real mess of his life and had undoubtedly caused his father much grief and sorrow. Yet the father did not look at his own hurts. The father saw his son returning and with great love *ran* to meet him where he was. Although the son asked to be received as a servant, the father called for the finest robe, a ring for his finger and sandals for his feet to be brought *quickly*. His accepting love did not want his son to grovel, even for a minute. The robe, the ring and the sandals clearly identified the young man, not as a servant, but as a beloved son. Then the father shared his great joy by holding a big welcome-home party.

This parable portrays not only the accepting love of God, but also the quality of agape love that seeks the highest good for the other individual. While the father's heart must have longed for his son, he did not send help to the distant country, which would have enabled the son to stay there. His love allowed the son to experience the consequences of his own actions. These consequences were a key factor in the son's return home.

This is how God's love reaches out to us. He will allow us to make a mess of our lives and to experience the difficult circumstances that come as a result. The painful consequences are allowed to draw us back to Himself. Then when God sees a repentant heart, He meets us right where we are. He doesn't wait for us to be mature and holy before His accepting love reaches out to receive us. He quickly accepts repentant sinners as His children; and because of His love, mercy and grace, He clothes us with His robes of righteousness.

GOD'S ACCEPTING LOVE TOUCHES ME

7.   Take a few moments to carefully examine your own heart. Perhaps you feel that you have made a mess of your life. Do you realize that God's love eagerly receives repentant sinners and will quickly accept you, even with your failures and shortcomings? His love longs to receive you into intimate fellowship as His own precious child. Write a paragraph thanking God for His love which sees beyond your faults and joyfully accepts you as His beloved child.

If you have difficulty fully believing that God's love will accept you, ask a trusted Christian friend to pray with you in this regard. It will be difficult for you to reach out in love to another unless you first feel the acceptance of God toward you. His love will eagerly accept you and He longs to draw you into His arms of love just as the father in this story loved and embraced his wayward son.

8. How do you relate to a prodigal? Perhaps you know someone who is making a real mess of his or her life. Consider the following questions:

   a. Are your actions in any way enabling the person to continue in sin? If yes, ask God to show you ways that your love can be a healthy love that will help to bring that sinner to repentance.
   b. Do your actions toward that individual more closely resemble the actions of the father in the parable or the actions of the older son?

   Ask God to show you ways that you can show loving acceptance while not enabling the person to continue in sin. Write down any ideas that He gives you.

REACHING OUT WITH LOVING ACCEPTANCE TO OTHERS

9. In Romans 14:1-12, what are we commanded to do in verse 1?

   Why are we commanded to accept others without judgment?

   What do verses 9-12 teach us about judging?
   Judge not.

   Why were these people judging each other (v. 5)?
   They were convinced in their own minds that they were right.

These people had a difference of opinion. Some, having come from a strong Jewish background, held certain days as sacred occasions, but these days held no special significance to the Gentile believers. There was also a question of whether the meat found in the markets had come from animals that had been used in sacrifice to pagan gods. As a result, some refrained from eating meat altogether. Others believed that since pagan gods had no power, there was no harm in eating meat and enjoying it. They thanked God for it. Both of these groups had chosen actions they felt would honor God and both were convinced they had chosen correctly.

Paul emphasized that because <u>both groups had chosen their actions in honor to God</u>, <u>He had accepted the actions of both</u>. A problem arose when one group did not accept the other. Instead, <u>they judged each other, not because their actions were wrong, but because they were different</u>.

List some current issues that might be similar to the questions of special days and unclean food as shown in this passage.

10. According to Romans 14:13-23, what attitudes do we need to demonstrate toward persons whose actions are different from ours (v. 13)?

How does verse 15 relate to the instructions in the second part of verse 13?

What important action of love is described in verses 15, 20 and 21?

List ways an individual's actions can destroy the work of God.

What are we commanded to do in verse 19?

List practical actions you could take that lead to peace and to building others up.

What is the proper relationship between freedom in Christ and love for each other?

In these verses Paul warned the Roman believers against judging God's servants. Just as you would not go into another person's business and begin to correct his employees, God doesn't want us judging or condemning His servants. That's neither our business nor our calling. At the same time, Paul urged that we conduct ourselves in such a manner that we will not cause others to stumble. If what we are doing in the exercise of our freedom in Christ causes another to stumble in his or her walk with the Lord, we are not acting out of love. We might need to limit our freedom to help another Christian who is weaker.

11. In Romans 15:1-7, what actions of love are described in verses 1 and 2?

How do the Scriptures help us during difficult times in our relationships with others (v. 4)?

What key to unity is found in verse 5 and how would this action build unity?

What does verse 7 command and what will be the result?

What does it mean to you to "accept one another as Christ has accepted you"?

Why do you think accepting one another will bring praise to Jesus?

Accepting weaknesses in others is not common to human nature. Our human nature wants others to change to fit our standards before we will accept them. Our natural tendency is to be critical and judgmental. Jesus, however, did not come into the world to condemn it (see John 3:17) and we are called to follow His example. A critical, condemning attitude pushes people away from us and from God. Accepting others with their faults will help to draw them to Jesus, allowing Him to change them. Following Jesus and gaining encouragement and hope from the Scriptures will help us accept others in spite of their weaknesses.

A Closer Look at My Own Heart

12. Take a few minutes to carefully examine your own heart regarding your ability to accept others. What characteristics do you find hardest to accept in others?

As you read the following passage, let God reveal truth to you regarding any judgmental tendencies you may have in your life.

13. From Luke 6:37-45, list the phrases in verses 37 and 38 that describe specific actions. What is the expected result of each action?

Action	Result

What do verses 41 and 42 teach us about condemning?

What do you think is meant by the statement, "For with the measure you use, it will be measured to you" (v. 38)?

How does that statement relate to love and acceptance?

To judgment and condemnation?

All of us want to be loved and accepted by others. It is important to realize that it is only as we love and accept others that they will love and accept us in return. If we are critical, condemning people, others will be critical and condemning of us. If we are loving and accepting, we are usually loved and accepted in return.

What important truth concerning our words and actions is found in Luke 6:45?

We want to respect people, but it is impossible to truly accept others until we change our way of thinking. We often come into relationships with unrealistic expectations. Instead of viewing people as sinners with shortcomings and faults just like ours, we somehow expect them to never fail us. When they ultimately do, we tend to make mental lists of the ways we have been hurt or disappointed. As we focus on their failures, our lists of grievances increase in magnitude and importance. Then, because we want to be loving, we try to speak or act with love and acceptance while still clinging to our hurts or disappointments. Unfortunately, it doesn't work. We fool no one. A person usually knows when you accept and respect him or her and can tell if you are insincere.

The only way we can treat a person with genuine respect and acceptance is to *change our way of thinking* about that individual. First, we need to give up unrealistic expectations. Then we need to ask God to show us how He sees that person and to show us his or her good qualities. We can take note of the good qualities and daily thank God for those good attributes. We can also begin to show appreciation to the person for the qualities that are commendable.

As we change our focus from the failures to the good qualities, we often find sincere feelings of respect and acceptance growing within us. Our actions toward that person will begin to demonstrate loving acceptance. As our actions and attitudes change, the other individual will usually sense that change and will feel free to grow and develop additional positive qualities.

Sometimes our expectations of ourselves are even more unrealistic than our expectations of others. We dislike ourselves because we can't live up to our own expectations. As we focus on our negative qualities, Satan gains more power to control us. Ask God to show you your positive qualities and begin to focus on strengthening them. God will build you up and as you mature, your good qualities will increase.

14. According to Philippians 4:8, what should be the focus of our minds?

Ask God to help you change the focus of your mind to the good.

Action Steps I Can Take Today

15. **Prayerfully ask God to show you your heart.** Write in your journal any insights that He gives you. Ask God to help you honestly answer the following:

   • In what ways am I treating others with acceptance?
   • In what ways am I judging or condemning others?

16. **Ask God to show you how He views a person that you are having difficulty accepting.** Ask God to reveal to you that person's good qualities and any areas where he or she may be hurting. Record in your journal what God reveals to you about that individual.

   Daily thank God for the good in that person and ask God to meet his or her needs. This will help you overcome any negative focus.

17. **Memorize and personalize Philippians 4:8.** Write it on a card and place the card where you can frequently be reminded of those things you need to focus upon. Daily choose to focus on that which is good.

- Four -

LOVE IS FORGIVING

Nothing in Marie wanted to forgive. The pain of an abusive childhood had taken its toll. She felt abandoned, abused, hurt and extremely angry. Fearing forgiveness would only open the door for more hurt, she fiercely hung on to her grievances. The unresolved anger and the unforgiveness eventually turned to bitter cynicism against people in general. She had difficulty relating to anyone. Marie's anger at her parents turned into anger at God. Why had He allowed such abuse and why did the abuse continue to devastate her life so many years later? It seemed the childhood abuse had destined her to a lifetime of misery.

A Closer Look at the Problem

We live in a world that is cursed by sin. As a result, some people seem to be deliberately abusive. Others, through their careless or thoughtless actions, can hurt our feelings, disappoint us and leave us wounded. The natural tendency is to refuse to forgive the offending individual. Unfortunately, unforgiveness and unresolved anger only prolong the pain, prevent healing and sabotage future relationships.

This chapter will show us that Jesus' love toward us is a forgiving love. If we are to love as Jesus loves us, we must also extend forgiveness to others. The threefold focus of this lesson is to…

1. Help us fully receive God's forgiveness toward us.
2. Show us how unresolved anger hinders forgiveness and illustrate practical steps to overcome that obstacle.
3. Teach us how to extend forgiveness toward others, even when we do not want to.

Before you begin your study, ask God to show you any areas of unforgiveness or unresolved anger in your own life. Ask Him to help you apply the truths of His Word to your own relationships.

A Closer Look at God's Truth

THE FORGIVING LOVE OF JESUS

1. In Matthew 9:1-8, why do you think Jesus addressed the man's need for forgiveness before He healed him?

   What does verse 6 teach us about Jesus and forgiveness?

   What did the man's healing demonstrate?

Though the religious leaders questioned Jesus' right to forgive, this passage clearly demonstrates both His willingness and His divine authority to do so.

2. According to John 8:3-11, in what sin had this woman become entangled and what punishment did the law prescribe for that sin?

What standard for condemning others did Jesus express in verse 7?

Why do you think the oldest of the accusers left first?

What does verse 11 teach us about Jesus' forgiveness?

The sad truth is that all of us sin and are in need of Jesus' forgiveness. It is easy to look at the sin of others and to feel smug or self-righteous. Jesus asked these accusers to examine themselves and as they did so, they saw their own sin. It is interesting that the older individuals were more quickly aware of the sin in their own lives than the younger ones.

Jesus wants us to also examine ourselves. As we become aware of our own sin, we are not so quick to condemn others. His love reaches out to the worst of sinners and He stands ready and willing to forgive. Then He asks that we leave our lives of sin and He empowers us to change.

3. From Matthew 26:67,68 and 27:26-31, list the ways that Jesus was mistreated.

4. According to Luke 23:32-34, how did Jesus react to the mistreatment He received?

Why was Jesus able to respond the way He did?

What effect do you think His forgiveness might have had on those who had mistreated Him?

In some mysterious way, forgiving seems to release the power of God to work in another's life. Notice that less than two months after Jesus had asked God to forgive those who had mistreated Him, 3,000 people were saved in one day (see Acts 2:41). Possibly many of those 3,000 were the same individuals who had been in Jerusalem screaming for Jesus' crucifixion. They had mocked Him, spit on Him and watched as He was crucified, but He asked God to forgive them. Love means forgiving. Jesus was able to respond to cruel mistreatment with the forgiveness that comes from unselfish love. His love, which manifested itself in forgiveness, had a life-changing effect on those for whom He prayed.

It is often difficult to forgive those who have hurt us. It is sometimes even harder to forgive those who have hurt the people we love. One way that we can develop a forgiving spirit is to choose to pray for that person who has caused the pain just as Jesus prayed for those who were hurting Him. When we pray for the person who has hurt us or those we love, forgiveness begins to grow within us. The anger loses its power and the hurts begin to heal as we pray for the offender.

5.   What does 1 John 1:8-10 teach about Jesus' forgiveness?

Just as Jesus forgave sin when He walked upon the earth, He still forgives all who will put their trust in Him. No matter how terrible our sin may be, we have the promise of 1 John 1:9: If we confess our sin, He will forgive and He will cleanse us. Christians do not have to be weighed down with guilt. We can claim the forgiveness of Jesus and realize that through accepting Him, we are holy and blameless in God's sight (see Ephesians 1:4,7).

6.   Take a few minutes to examine your own heart. If you have any uncon-fessed sin standing between you and God, confess it right now. Then claim the forgiveness that is yours in Christ Jesus. Thank God that He sees you as holy and blameless because of Jesus' sacrifice of love. If you have difficulty believing that God can or would forgive you, ask a mature Christian to pray with you in this regard.

EXTENDING FORGIVENESS TO OTHERS

7.   According to Colossians 3:12-14, what character qualities do God's people need to exhibit?

What instructions are given regarding forgiveness?

Describe what you think it means to "forgive as the Lord forgave you" (v. 13).

What quality needs to be added to bring perfect unity?

8. What does Matthew 6:14,15 teach about forgiving others and receiving forgiveness from God?

It is important to realize that a bitter, unforgiving spirit shows a serious break in our relationship with God. Those who will not forgive others cannot experience the forgiveness of God. As a result, the unforgiving person will often have tremendous feelings of guilt. As long as we refuse to forgive, we continue to experience the hurts, leaving the door open for Satan to outwit us (see 2 Corinthians 2:5-11). An unforgiving heart is dangerous, not only damaging the person who is unforgiven, but the one who refuses to forgive as well. When we choose forgiveness, we free God to begin His work of healing in our lives.

9. Take a few moments to ask God to show you any lack of forgiveness that is hindering your relationship with Him or with others. Record in your journal what God shows you. Write a prayer asking Him to help you want to forgive that other person. Remember that He wants you to forgive and He will empower you to do it.

HOW UNRESOLVED ANGER HINDERS FORGIVENESS

It is clear that Scripture commands us to forgive, and those who have forgiven clearly testify of the freedom and healing that forgiveness brings. One of the primary hindrances to forgiveness and to feelings of love is unresolved anger. In fact, unresolved anger in one relationship will often hinder your ability to love in another relationship. For example, unresolved anger toward a parent often hinders one's ability to love a spouse. Let's look at what Scripture teaches about the dangers of anger.

10. In Ephesians 4:25-32, what instructions does Paul give regarding anger?

What does the phrase "in your anger, do not sin" (v. 26) imply about anger?

Anger is a natural human emotion that in itself is not sin. Even Jesus, the perfect Son of God, expressed anger (see Mark 3:5; 10:14) and the Old Testament often speaks of God's anger against sin and injustice. Anger is an intense emotion during which our physical bodies produce extra adrenaline. This adrenaline surge makes anger a very powerful emotion that can be used in healthy and constructive ways, but more often results in sinful and destructive behavior. Because anger is such an intense emotion, we need to be aware of its dangerous potential. What we do with our anger determines whether or not it becomes sin.

What sinful tendency in handling anger does Ephesians 4:26 warn against?

What is the result of the improper handling of anger (v. 27)?

How can holding on to anger give Satan a foothold in our lives?

What guidelines regarding our speech are given in verse 29?

How can those guidelines help us resolve anger?

Because anger is such an intense emotion, the potential for hurtful or abusive speech is significant. As Paul deals with this critical issue, he warns against unwholesome talk that tears people down, rather than building them up. What we say and how we say it will often play a key role in determining whether a relationship is restored or damaged further. Words that are beneficial to others will help restore relationships.

What are we urged to avoid in Ephesians 4:30?

How can inappropriate handling of anger grieve the Holy Spirit?

What sinful tendencies in handling anger are we urged to eliminate (v. 31)?

This passage clearly points out some of the ways in which anger can and does become sinful. If we hang onto anger and do not resolve it quickly, it easily turns into bitterness and will greatly hinder our ability to love. In much the same way, if our anger leads to abusive talk, rage, brawling, slander or malice, the anger has clearly become sinful and destructive to relationships. Anger is a hindrance to love and we must learn to deal with it in healthy ways.

11. According to Psalm 39:1-3, what good intentions did David have in keeping silent?

What was the unfortunate result of suppressing his anger?

Knowing the dangerous potential of expressing anger, many Christians (like David) try to refrain from expressing their negative emotions altogether. Unfortunately, burying anger usually results in increased anguish just as David experienced. Unspoken and unresolved anger eats away at the soul, distorting our perspective and destroying our ability to love. Communication is often a key to working through the conflict, resolving the anger and coming into a healthy relationship.

12. According to Ephesians 4:15, what important principle do we need to apply to relationships?

What will be the result?

When expressing anger, we need to carefully apply the principle of "speaking the truth in love" (v. 15). Words spoken in anger have tremendous potential to destroy because they attack the one who is the object of the anger. We must learn to express our hurts and feelings without attacking. We must also be sensitive to the hurts the other person may be experiencing. It is vital that we talk *and* listen to each other.

When attempting to resolve anger, we first need to pray; then in an attitude of humility and kindness we need to go to the other person involved. We need to realize that *we* may have also inflicted pain on that person. We must take responsibility for our role in the conflict and ask forgiveness for any pain we might have caused. If we only confront by voicing our hurts and disappointments, we might get rid of our anger, but in the process we leave the other individual feeling bitter and angry. God's plan is that we be united by a love that forgives, rather than being divided by anger.

A Closer Look at My Own Heart

How important is it that we forgive? Most people want to love and desire healthy relationships. Regrettably, many who desire loving relationships still hold on to areas of unforgiveness because they fear that forgiveness will open the door for additional pain.

To forgive does not mean we cannot take a stand against future sin nor set some healthy boundaries. Remember that agape love always seeks the highest good for the other individual, and setting healthy boundaries may be in the best interest of everyone involved. Likewise, forgiveness does not mean pretending we were not hurt. Often we must acknowledge the hurt and take it to God before we can really forgive from the heart.

As you study the following passages, ask God to show you the importance of forgiveness in your relationships. Take a few moments and ask God to show you any unresolved anger or lack of forgiveness with which you need to deal.

13. What question did Peter ask in Matthew 18:21,22?

What does the question show about Peter?

How many times did Jesus say we should forgive?

Peter may have asked the question regarding how many times he needed to forgive to justify not having to forgive in the future. Perhaps he had already forgiven seven times and felt that was sufficient. Although translators differ as to whether Jesus told Peter to forgive 77 times (*NIV*) or 70 times 7 (*KJV, NEB, RSV*), Jesus was most likely implying that Peter needed to quit counting and keep on forgiving. Perhaps God is also asking you to do the same.

14.   Read Matthew 18:23-27. How much did the first servant owe the king?

What did the king order to repay the debt (v. 25)?

How did the servant react to this order (v. 26)?

How did the king respond to the servant's plea (v. 27)?

It is important to note that 10,000 talents represented an enormous amount of money, equal to millions of dollars in today's economy. There was no way this servant would ever have been able to repay such a huge debt. It was only the goodness of a merciful master that totally cancelled the debt and set him free.

15.   Read Matthew 18:28-35. How much did the fellow servant owe the first servant?

In contrast to the huge debt the first servant owed, the 100 denarii represented only a few dollars.

How did he treat the man who owed him the relatively small sum of money?

What effect did his lack of forgiveness have on the man who owed him?

How did the fellow servants respond to what they saw?

How was the master affected?

How did this man's lack of forgiveness destroy him?

Just as the lack of his own willingness to forgive left this ungrateful man tortured and imprisoned, people who refuse to forgive find themselves in tormented bondage. The consequences of not forgiving are widespread and severe. This man's lack of forgiveness impacted the one owing him money, his fellow servants and the king. However, the one most severely affected was the man himself. The master had given him freedom, but because of *his* own unforgiving attitude, that freedom was taken away and he was placed in prison.

Because God in His mercy has forgiven us, He expects us to be merciful and forgiving toward others. Refusal to forgive leaves us locked in the pain and unable to experience freedom in Christ. The most unhappy people on earth are those who will not forgive. Hanging onto our grievances always carries severe consequences.

16.   What consequence of not forgiving is found in Matthew 18:35?

This verse points out the terrible spiritual consequences of refusing to forgive. Those who refuse to forgive are unable to relate to God because of the bitterness in their hearts and often that bitterness is passed on to children and grandchildren. In addition, there are physical and emotional consequences because the lack of forgiveness creates a greater susceptibility toward illnesses and depression. Regrettably, there are also social consequences; the bitterness toward one person will hinder your relationship with another, and you will tend to become like the one you resent. Failing to forgive prevents the emotional and spiritual healing of the hurts and surrenders the power to attain happiness in your life to the offender.

The good news is that we can *choose* to forgive. With God's help, we can gain the power we need to enable us to forgive from the depths of our innermost being. We do not have to *feel* like forgiving before we forgive. If we wait for feelings, we will never forgive! We forgive because it is required by God and because it is in our own best interest.

Action Steps I Can Take Today

17. Determine to quickly resolve anger in healthy ways. The following practical steps can be used any time you are having difficulty resolving anger:

    a. **Give yourself permission to express anger in healthy ways.**

    b. **Identify the root emotion.** Anger is a secondary emotion. Often what we're feeling is hurt, fear, embarrassment, etc.

    c. **Give yourself time for the intensity of the anger to dissipate** before addressing the situation. If we react too quickly, we may say or do things in the heat of the moment that will damage the relationship and lead to regret.

    d. **Do something physical to dissipate the adrenaline** such as taking a brisk walk or jog, working in the yard, etc. This will help you to be in better control when you ultimately express the anger.

    e. **Ask for God's help in resolving the situation.** Praying aloud may be especially helpful in working through the intensity of the emotion before addressing the situation.

    f. **Express the anger in healthy ways.** This means calmly expressing the anger at the action without attacking the person. Express the primary emotion that you felt, (i. e., fear, hurt, etc.) and avoid use of the words "always" and "never."

    g. **Forgive the offender.**

18. Take the following steps toward forgiveness:

    a. **Choose to forgive.** Remember that forgiveness is a decision that we make to obey God. If you will set your will to forgive, God will give the emotional strength to be able to forgive from the heart.

    b. **Ask God to show you what He wants you to learn from this situation.** God has allowed this situation for some purpose and He will bring good from every difficulty in our lives if we will let Him. Record in your journal anything God reveals to you.

    c. **Ask God for His power to forgive.** Sometimes you may need to ask God for the desire to forgive, but remember that forgiveness is His will for you and that He will give you the grace and the power to do it when you sincerely ask for His help. Write a prayer requesting this power in your journal.

    d. **Pray for the offender.** Ask God to show you how you can best pray for this person and record what He shows you in your journal. Pray for the individual any time feelings of anger or hurt resurface.

    e. **Ask God to show you if you need to express forgiveness to the other individual.** Sometimes this is helpful and at other times it may cause the other person more pain. Seek godly counsel from a mature Christian if you are unsure of God's direction.

    f. **Thank God for the freedom and the forgiveness that is yours through Jesus Christ our Lord.**

- Five -

LOVE IS SACRIFICING AND SERVING

As the pastor paid tribute to his deceased mother, he said, "It was not until I was an adult that I realized her favorite piece of chicken was not the neck." Raised in a large family during the depression era, meat was not plentiful on their table. When the chicken was passed around, his mother always took the neck. She took it so graciously that he did not realize that she was putting the needs of the family above her own. He thought the almost meatless neck was simply her favorite piece. In many ways his mother had loved with a sacrificing and serving love that cheerfully placed the needs of others above her own.

A Closer Look at the Problem

We live in a society that has been trained to look out for self, to make meeting *my* wants and *my* needs the number-one priority in life. Desiring positions of prominence and power, we hope the recognition of our importance will bring the feelings of significance that every individual longs for. Serving where there seems to be little recognition or thanks is difficult and seemingly unrewarding.

In sharp contrast to a self-centered society is the sacrificial and serving love of Jesus toward us. He left the splendors of heaven to face rejection, to suffer and ultimately to die, in order to meet our greatest need. His kind of love is never self-centered nor arrogant. If we are to love as Jesus loves us, we must also learn to love with a love that is willing to serve and to give sacrificially. The threefold focus for this lesson is to…

1. Recognize and appreciate the sacrificial love of Jesus toward us.
2. See how Jesus gave us an example of serving love in action.
3. Learn how we can overcome the natural tendency toward self-ishness and reach out to others with a serving and sacrificial love.

As you begin your study, ask God to open your heart to more fully grasp His love which will empower you to love others. Ask Him to help you recognize any areas of selfishness that are hindering the growth of love in your life.

A Closer Look at God's Truth

JESUS' SACRIFICING LOVE

1. In John 15:9-15, what does Jesus promise those who keep His commands?

What did Jesus command us to do (v. 12)?

What does Jesus describe as the greatest expression of love?

How is Jesus' entire life a demonstration of that kind of love?

2. Read 1 John 4:9-12. How did God show His love for us (v. 9)?

How does verse 10 define love?

What should be the result of receiving God's great love for us (v. 11)?

What does it show when we love each other?

How does accepting God's love make it easier to love one another?

Jesus gave up the glory and the adoration that was His in heaven to become one of us. His love brought Him to earth that we might enjoy abundant and eternal life. He was rejected, beaten, spit upon, mocked and crucified to enable us to come into a right relationship with God. His willingness to bear excruciating physical pain and to carry the unspeakable shame of mankind's sin and guilt demonstrates His incredible love for us. When we accept Jesus as Savior and Lord, His love becomes active within us. As we allow His Spirit to control us, His love at work in us willingly reaches out to others with sacrificial love.

3. Read Ephesians 5:1,2. What instructions are given in verse 1?

Describe what you think it means to imitate God as His "dearly loved children."

What kind of life are we to live?

How are we instructed to love?

How does loving with a sacrificial love relate to being an imitator of God?

Children are fantastic imitators, loving to play dress-up and pretend they are Mommy or Daddy. Through imitation, they quickly master language skills and often reflect their parents' behavior. In the same way, God wants our lives to imitate His expression of sacrificial love toward us.

List some practical actions of sacrificial love that can be demonstrated in today's culture.

How would sacrificial love relate to the use of your time?

Your money?

Your home and other possessions?

Your energy?

The term "sacrificial" implies there is a significant cost involved in what one is giving. This usually means giving beyond what is comfortable and easy for us. People who are hungry for love and attention may need more of our time or energy than we can comfortably give. Sacrificial love may require that we open our homes, share our finances or in some other way become involved in meeting their needs. Sacrificial love must be accomplished in and through the power of Jesus. Attempting to love sacrificially in one's own strength too often results in fatigue, resentment and burnout.

THE SERVING LOVE OF JESUS

4. In John 13:1-5, what did Jesus know according to verse 1?

What did He show His disciples?

What was Jesus' position and authority?

What action of love did Jesus perform?

What did Jesus' washing of the disciples' feet show?

How does His willingness to become a servant relate to His greatness?

As Jesus ate with His disciples on the night before He was to be crucified, there was much they needed to learn about true greatness. As humans, they were prone to the common practice of comparing themselves with each other and wanted to hold the most important positions in the Savior's kingdom.

The task of washing the feet was traditionally done by the lowliest of the household servants and none of the disciples appeared willing to do such a menial task. Yet Jesus, the Lord and Master, showed His great love to His disciples by taking the position of the lowliest servant and performing the humblest of acts.

5. Luke 22:24-27 records a discussion that took place that very same night. What was the subject of the dispute?

According to these verses, how do the Gentiles (or unbelievers) view greatness?

How are Christians to be different in their views of greatness?

Describe what you think Jesus meant when He said, "The greatest among you should be like the youngest, and the one who rules like the one who serves" (v. 26).

How did Jesus describe Himself (v. 27)?

Perhaps the disciples' discussion prompted Jesus' practical demonstration of servant love. He contrasted the world's view of greatness, in which power and prominence appear to equal greatness, with God's view, in which serving others denotes greatness. In a culture that honored the elderly, the youngest would have been the one who traditionally served the others and would have been considered the least significant. By contrast, Jesus indicated the greatest in His kingdom would be the one who willingly serves others.

6. Read John 13:12-17. What had the disciples called Jesus?

What was His response to those titles (v. 13)?

What instructions did Jesus give (vv. 14,15)?

What truth was Jesus emphasizing in verse 16?

What promise is given for those who obey these instructions?

How does this passage apply to Christians today?

What are some practical ways that we can serve each other?

How do you feel when you do something to help another?

In washing the disciples' feet, Jesus gave all believers a beautiful example of love in action. Love willingly becomes a servant. Love does not seek to exalt self, but to serve others. Rather than asking, *How much must I do?* serving love asks, *What more can I do?*

We often try to exalt ourselves just as the disciples did. Verse 17 emphasizes that it is as we serve others that we are blessed. When we serve others, our own sense of self-worth grows. It is in humbling ourselves and serving others that we are exalted.

7. From Matthew 25:31-40, list the phrases commending those who were to inherit the kingdom (vv. 34-36).

   Why did the words of the King surprise those who had served others (vv. 37-39)?

   How did Jesus view those actions done for others?

   How might verse 40 be a motivation for us to serve others?

8. From Matthew 25:41-46, list phrases telling what these individuals had failed to do.

   How did Jesus view their lack of action?

It is interesting that neither group in this parable thought of their service or lack of service as unto Jesus, but that is the way He described both. The first group was not saved through their actions, but their loving service to others demonstrated God's Spirit at work within them. The lack of loving actions in the second group showed they did not really even know God. They thought they did, but their lack of genuine concern proved otherwise.

9. How does Galatians 5:13 instruct us regarding our use of freedom and its relationship to love? *Not to use freedom to sin, but love.*

Through Jesus' loving sacrifice, we have been set free from the power of sin and the burden of legalism. However, that freedom should never be used as an excuse for sinful behavior. Instead, we are called to serve each other in love. In Galatians 5:13 the Greek word translated "love" is once again *agape*, which denotes a giving, serving love that always seeks the highest good for the other individual.

A Closer Look at My Own Heart

For most of us, sacrificial giving or joyfully serving others does not come naturally. Yet there is tremendous power in this kind of love. As you study the remaining passages, ask God to show you how applying the principles given in these verses would affect your relationships. Ask Him to show you changes in attitudes and actions that would help you to grow in Christlike love.

If you are struggling to love another person, ask God to show you ways that you can serve that person. As you willingly seek to serve and to meet that person's needs, your feelings are given an atmosphere of love in which to grow.

10. As you read Philippians 2:1-11, list the actions and attitudes that are encouraged. (**Note:** the Greek word translated "if" in verse 1 can also be translated "since.")

Which of these actions and attitudes are strengths for you?

What attitudes and actions are discouraged?

any interruption — ordained by God.

Which are weaknesses that point to areas of needed growth?

How is Jesus described in verse 6?

List phrases that show what Jesus became for us.

Which phrases show that Jesus had a choice?

What qualities was Paul encouraging when he urged the Philippians (and us) to have the same attitude that Jesus had?

How does this passage relate to the renewing of the mind (see Romans 12:1,2)?

List practical actions you can take to renew your mind and develop Christlike attitudes.

How would your relationships be changed if you were to use Philippians 2:3-8 as your guide?

What changes do you need to make to put these verses into practice?

How did God reward the sacrificial and serving actions of Jesus?

Jesus' actions are the ultimate example of sacrificial and serving love. Sometimes it is difficult for us to serve others or to serve in lowly positions because we feel it lessens our significance as individuals. The struggle for feelings of significance and importance may hinder our willingness to serve others. By contrast, Jesus knew full well who and what He was. Lacking any struggle regarding His own identity and significance, He was able to freely serve others.

It will be difficult to respond with Jesus' kind of love unless we first recognize who and what we are in Jesus. We are God's deeply loved children, so valuable to Him that He sent His Son to bring us into a right relationship with Himself. As we more fully grasp how precious we are to God, He assures us of our personal significance and importance. Then He works in us to develop the same attitudes that Jesus had. This involves spending time with Him, feeding on His Word and allowing His Holy Spirit the freedom to change our way of thinking. We must honestly look at our self-seeking and self-serving attitudes and ask God to change our hearts.[1]

Often when struggling in a relationship, part of the problem is that we allow our minds to dwell on our own unmet needs. Focusing on our unfulfilled needs tends to magnify their importance and we become increasingly dissatisfied in our relationships. Changing our focus from *our* unmet needs to honestly seeking to do what will be best for others and meeting their true needs is necessary for a healthy relationship.

When we seek to meet the needs of others, we will often find our own needs are also being met or God will graciously change our needs to bring us peace and satisfaction in any situation. By contrast, if we make meeting our needs our number one priority, those needs will rarely be met and we will continue to feel unsatisfied. When we seek to meet the needs of others, we usually find joy, contentment and feelings of love growing within us.

Actions Steps I Can Take Today

11. **Spend time praising God that He sees you as significant and extremely valuable.** Remember, it was His great love for us that led to the sacrificial death of Jesus. To help you more fully accept your personal significance,

read the following passages and record in your journal what each says about your position in Christ:

John 1:12	Romans 8:1,2	Romans 8:35-39
1 Corinthians 6:19,20	Ephesians 2:4-6	Ephesians 2:18,19

Thank Him that the truth indicated in each of these passages is true for you.

12. **Ask God to show you any actions or attitudes that demonstrate selfishness in your relationships.** Record in your journal what He reveals to you.

13. **In your journal, write a prayer giving God permission to change those attitudes and actions.** Ask Him to renew your mind and help you grow in Christlike attitudes and actions.

14. **Recognize that actions that convey love to you may not necessarily convey love to another individual.** If you are seeking to strengthen a love relationship, consider asking the other person, "What communicates love to you?" Then determine to act upon what you learn.

15. **Ask God to show you specific actions of serving love that He wants you to perform.** Make a list of the actions He shows you; then record the date you perform each serving act.

Note:

1. For additional study on renewing your mind, see the Aglow Bible Study by Sharon A. Steele, *Choosing to Change* (Ventura, CA: Gospel Light, 1998).

Six

LOVE IS KIND AND UPLIFTING

Emotionally beaten down and never affirmed in his early childhood, Brian had responded by withdrawing into himself and believing that he was very stupid. Later he was sent to live with grandparents who lovingly accepted him. They showered him with kindness and their words affirmed his value. Gradually the wounds began to heal and he wrote a letter declaring "I'm not stupid anymore." The power of loving-kindness had touched his life and built him up.

A Closer Look at the Problem

Life is sometimes cruel and painful. Disappointments can overwhelm, leaving one feeling inadequate and insignificant. At such difficult times, kind words and deeds can sustain and bring hope. Everyone wants to be treated with kindness and without it life becomes painful and burdensome.

In this chapter we will see that Jesus' love demonstrates kindness. If we are to love as Jesus loves us, treating others kindly is essential. Sometimes this is easy and other times it may be extremely difficult. One of the most needed acts of kindness is that of building each other up. The sinful nature is quick to attack and tear others down, leaving individuals struggling with low self-esteem. They need someone who will reach out to them with kindness and uplifting. The dual focus of this lesson is to...

1. Recognize and accept the loving-kindness of the Lord toward us.
2. Choose words and actions of kindness which will reach out to others with love that builds them up.

Before you begin, ask God to make you aware of any unkindness toward others in your life. Will you ask Him to teach you how to replace unkind words and deeds with actions that are kind and uplifting?

A Closer Look at God's Truth

GOD'S KINDNESS TOWARD US

1. In Jeremiah 31:3,4, how is God's love described?

2. As you read 1 Corinthians 13:4-7, list the actions that describe kindnesses.

3. How did Jesus' love demonstrate kindness in the following passages?

   Matthew 19:13-15

   Mark 5:25-34

   Luke 5:12,13

4. What do the following verses reveal about God's love and His kindness?

   Psalm 63:3

   Ephesians 2:4-7

   Titus 3:4-7

List ways you have personally benefited from God's loving-kindness toward you.

As you more fully grasp the nature of God's love for you, you will find greater freedom to risk loving others with kindness that will build them up. If you have difficulty believing that God is kind or that He directs His kindness toward you, ask a more mature Christian to pray with you in this regard.

GOD'S KINDNESS TOUCHES OTHERS THROUGH HIS CHILDREN

5.   According to 2 Peter 1:3,4, what has God in His kindness given to us?

What key to power is described in verse 3?

How do verses 3 and 4 promise the strength to live a life of love?

What role does God's Spirit play in living that life of victory?

What do you think the phrase "through our knowledge of him" means (v. 3)?

How can we grow in our knowledge of Him?

To those who personally know Jesus as Savior and Lord, God promises everything we need to live a life of godliness. This means His divine power at work in us enables us to rise above the world's corruption and live a life of love. To grow in our knowledge of Him, we must spend time with Him, sharing our struggles and listening to His voice. Spending time studying His Word will help us know His heart and as we obey His voice, we will grow in our knowledge of Him (see John 14:21).

6. In 2 Peter 1:5-9, which phrase indicates the individual's responsibility in Christian growth?

What character qualities need to be added to faith?

Which phrase in verse 8 implies a growing Christian?

What is the result of these qualities growing in our lives?

What steps can we take to add these qualities to our lives and help them to grow?

How does unkindness keep a Christian from being effective and productive?

How can kindness increase our effectiveness?

Even though God has given us everything we need to live a godly life, part of the responsibility for growth rests upon us. Growth is not automatic and we must do our part to grow in godly attributes. If we will draw into His presence and submit ourselves to Him, we will increase in our knowledge of Him and will grow in godliness. Our ability to treat others with loving-kindness will increase as we more fully grasp His great love for us.

7. What qualities does 2 Timothy 2:22-24 say we should pursue?

Describe ways an individual could pursue these qualities.

Why is it important to pursue these qualities "along with those who call on the Lord out of a pure heart" (v. 22)?

What kinds of arguments are we to avoid and why?

Do you feel all arguments are foolish and stupid? Why or why not?

What is the difference between an argument and a quarrel?

How can quarreling lead to unkindness and resentfulness?

How can quarreling make one's teaching ineffective?

When the apostle Paul wrote to the young Timothy, he shared principles that would help him succeed as an effective pastor and teacher. In urging Timothy to pursue righteousness, faith, love and peace, Paul implies that these important qualities are somewhat elusive and achieving them will require effort.

Foolish arguments will quickly undermine the growth of these godly qualities. Arguments in and of themselves are not necessarily foolish. For example, the apostle Paul often presented arguments proving Jesus was the Messiah (see Acts 9:22; 17:2-4; 18:4). However, there are many unnecessary arguments over inconsequential matters that lead to quarreling. The Greek word translated as "quarrels" in these verses implies anger and strife. These types of arguments need to be avoided as they are destructive to the kingdom of God.

What qualities does 2 Timothy 2:24 say the Lord's servant should possess?

In your life, who are the people that you are teaching?

Why is kindness so important if you are going to be an effective teacher?

Paul also urged kindness in all of God's servants. Kindness is an essential factor in our effectiveness as teachers, whether in our churches, jobs or homes. We need to realize that every Christian has a realm of influence and we are teaching through our attitudes, our words and our actions.

Unfortunately, too often our attitudes and actions are contrary to what we are trying to teach with our words. When this is true, our teachings become hollow and ineffective. For example, a child will be far more receptive to learning spiritual truths from a kind parent than from one who is unkind. The effectiveness of anyone who is trying to teach about God will be limited unless that individual's teaching is combined with actions of kindness. Regrettably, a lack of kindness in the teacher often leads to rejection of the teaching altogether.

8. In Titus 2:3-5, what was Titus encouraged to teach the older women?

What were the older women to teach the younger women?

What would be the result of the women learning these things?

What do you think is meant by the phrase "so that no one will malign the word of God" (v. 5)?

How do unkind actions bring disrespect to God?

How does kindness bring God glory?

THE POWER OF WORDS

Kindness is described in Scripture as both an action of love and a fruit of the Spirit (see 1 Corinthians 13:4 and Galatians 5:22). One important way we can express kindness is through loving words. As you study the following passages, let God speak to you regarding the impact of your words.

9.   According to 1 Corinthians 8:1, what does love do?

How does that action relate to our words?

10.   In 1 Thessalonians 5:8-11, what qualities are we encouraged to have?

What words imply these qualities are a protection?

How can we increase in those qualities?

What actions should be a result of God's love toward us (v. 11)?

What are some practical ways to apply the instructions in verse 11?

How does verse 11 relate to our words?

11. What do the following verses teach us about the power of our words?

Proverbs 12:18

Proverbs 15:1

Proverbs 15:4

Proverbs 16:24

Proverbs 18:21

2 Timothy 2:16

Words can be loving and kind, or they can be brutal and destructive. Words can build up, or they can tear down. Often those people who are the most difficult to love are those with low self-esteem. They are incapable of reaching out in love to others because they do not love themselves. One of the most needed actions of love toward those people is the need to build them up.

If you know such a person, ask God to show you his or her actions for which you can honestly be grateful. Tell that individual how much you appreciate each of the good qualities that God shows you. Expressing appreciation in this way will help you to focus upon the best in that person and it will encourage and build him or her up.

A Closer Look at My Own Heart

12. Take a few moments to honestly evaluate your own speech. Ask yourself the following questions:

- Does my speech usually bring healing or does it often wound?
- Does it bring life or does it crush the spirit?
- Do my words turn away wrath or do they stir up anger?
- Is my speech godless chatter that leads to greater ungodliness?
- Are my words pleasant or harsh?

Ask God to show you areas of needed improvement as you study the following:

13. According to Ephesians 4:29-32, what kind of talk should not come out of your mouth?

What should our words accomplish (v. 29)?

What actions of love are described in verse 32?

When do our words grieve the Holy Spirit?

How do verses 31 and 32 relate to our words?

Write a paraphrase of verses 29 through 32, personalizing these instructions to make them applicable to your life and your words.

As you make the building up of another person your goal, that person often begins to feel better about him- or herself and often that individual becomes easier to love. When you seek to build another person up, God will also give you increased feelings of love toward that person. Will you choose today to reach out to others with a love that is kind and builds up?

Action Steps I Can Take Today

14. **Take time to consider God's loving-kindness toward you.** In your journal, make a list of the different ways God has shown kindness to you and your loved ones. Then write a prayer of praise thanking God for His loving-kindness.

15. **Evaluate your recent conversations.** Think back over your conversations of the past week. In your journal, list times that your conversation has been helpful to others and times when it has been harmful.

    Ask God to reveal to you any areas of unwholesome talk in your life and record in your journal the areas that God reveals to you. Write a prayer confessing that unwholesome talk as sin and asking God to give you His strength to overcome.

16. **Ask God to give you a specific plan** to make your speech more beneficial and useful in building others up. Consider how you can apply the following practical suggestions to help you overcome unwholesome talk:

    - **Ask God's help daily.** Remember that no man can tame the tongue, but God's Holy Spirit can!
    - **Don't speak too quickly.** Carefully weigh what you will say.
    - **Speak in ways you want others to speak to you.**
    - **Pretend the recipient is a respected friend or your pastor.**
    - **Think how you would feel if your conversation were being recorded.**
    - **Refuse to participate in destructive conversation**, even as a listener.
    - **Ask yourself,** *What would Jesus say?*

- **Carefully guard what goes into your mind** because "Out of the over-flow of the heart the mouth speaks" (Matthew 12:34).

Record in your journal what you plan to do to make your speech more beneficial.

17. **Ask God to show you someone who needs your encouragement today** and to reveal practical ways that you can build that person up. Write in your journal any thoughts God reveals to you; then choose to follow His leading. As you respond to God's leading, record the dates along with the actions you are taking.

18. **Ask God to show you practical acts of kindness** that you can do to help build up and encourage the following people:

Your family members

Your friends

Your fellow workers

Others in your church or fellowship

19. **Memorize Psalm 19:14** and make it your daily prayer:

May the words of my mouth and the meditation of my heart be pleasing in your sight, O LORD, my Rock and my Redeemer.

Seven

LOVE IS DISCERNING

Jim and Louise loved their wayward daughter Karen and grieved as they watched her descend into the pit of drug and alcohol addiction. Repeatedly, they tried to help, paying bills, caring for her children and covering for her irresponsible behavior. Unfortunately, their efforts did not help Karen out of her addiction but instead enabled her to stay there. While their love may have been giving, serving and sacrificing, it was lacking in discernment. Eventually they realized how their actions were contributing to the problem. Jim and Louise arranged an intervention after which Karen voluntarily entered a treatment center and gained victory over the addiction. Karen needed love that was discerning.

A Closer Look at the Problem

Sometimes love needs to be tough and confrontive. It's easy to identify certain actions such as serving, sacrificing and accepting as actions of love. However, we see that God's love will also confront sin because it is in the best interest of the individual. Discerning love sometimes must say no and set healthy boundaries. Agape love that always seeks the highest good for the other individual is a discerning love that will recognize when a person needs tenderness or firmness. The dual focus of this chapter is to…

1. Discover how God's love toward us is a discerning love.
2. Help us grow in discernment so that our love will result in the highest good for the other individual.

Before you begin your study, will you ask God to show you areas where your love needs to grow in discernment? Will you ask Him to help you apply the truths from these scriptures to your relationships?

A Closer Look at God's Truth

1. In Mark 10:17-22, what did this young man's question reveal about himself?

Why do you think Jesus directed the man's attention to the commandments?

What does verse 20 reveal about the young man?

Notice that verse 21 says specifically that Jesus "loved him." How did Jesus' love show discernment?

What did Jesus promise if the young man would put God's kingdom first?

What did the young man choose and what was the result of his choice?

In this passage a rich young man who was also a ruler (see Luke 18:18) approached Jesus seeking the key to eternal life. Not only was the influential young man wealthy, but he appears to have lived a clean and wholesome life. His parents were probably proud to have him as a son. He had a genuine desire to be right with God but regretfully did not recognize his own sinfulness. In loving discernment Jesus truthfully confronted him with the change that was essential before he could be right with God. Riches had become more important to him than his relationship with God. Although Jesus loved the young man, He did not lessen his requirements for discipleship. The young man left full of sorrow, knowing that his riches and influence could not bring the peace and the joy he was seeking.

2. In Hebrews 12:4-11, what do verses 5 and 6 teach us about God's love?

How should we respond to God's discipline?

What does it show when God does not discipline an individual (v. 8)?

How does God's discipline compare to the discipline of a loving parent (vv. 9,10)?

What are the goals of God's discipline (vv. 9-11)?

How does this passage demonstrate the discerning nature of God's love?

The Greek verb which is translated as "discipline" in the *New International Version* properly relates to the training of a child and includes instruction, counsel, discipline, correction and chastisement as needed. God's discerning love will allow His children to experience consequences of wrong actions to draw us back to Himself. His love will let us go through difficult and painful circumstances because that is when we are the most likely to grow and mature.

His love, which always seeks our good, will bring correction to His children when needed.

The following passages tell of a situation in which the apostle Paul had to use a discerning and confronting love.

3. According to 1 Corinthians 5:1-6, what sin was Paul confronting?

What had been the attitude of the church (vv. 2,6)?

What attitudes should they have had?

What disciplinary action did Paul urge them to take in regard to this man (vv. 2,5)?

What was the goal of the discipline that Paul recommended (vv. 5,6)?

Why do you think Paul urged such drastic treatment of the sinning man?

How does sexual immorality destroy the work of the Lord?

Paul wrote to the Corinthians with a heavy heart. Corinth was notorious for its sexual promiscuity and religious prostitution, yet the church in Corinth had allowed blatant immorality of such an extreme nature that even the pagan Corinthians were shocked. The church had failed to confront the sinning individual and had proudly acted as if nothing were wrong. Paul urged prompt confrontation for the good of the individual and for the sake of the church. Paul expressed concern that this sin could easily spread to the entire fellowship.

Notice that there are actually two instances of confrontation in this passage. While Paul urged the church to deal with this man's sin, he also confronted the church regarding their attitudes and their lack of disciplinary action.

The following passages will show the results of these confrontations.

THE POSITIVE EFFECTS OF LOVING CONFRONTATION

4. In 2 Corinthians 7:2-7, which words express Paul's love for the Corinthians (v. 3)?

How does he affirm them (v. 4)?

How does Paul describe himself in verses 5 and 6?

Why do you think Paul was in such turmoil?

What had comforted Paul (vv. 6,7)?

When Paul arrived in Macedonia, he had no idea how the Corinthian church had reacted to his letter. Not knowing whether they had responded to his plea or had angrily rebelled against his instructions, he experienced great inner turmoil. Then Titus arrived from Corinth, bringing the good news of the powerful and positive impact of Paul's letter and assuring him of their love. This news brought the apostle great comfort and joy.

5. According to 2 Corinthians 7:8-11, what was the initial reaction to Paul's letter?

Why do you think Paul struggled with feelings of regret?

What had the Corinthians' sorrow led them to do?

What is the difference between "worldly sorrow" and "godly sorrow" (v. 10)?

What had the godly sorrow produced (vv. 10,11)?

When Paul addressed the blatant sin in the church, it was necessary for him to be stern. Many Bible scholars feel a third letter, harshly written to the Corinthians (but lost to us), may be the letter Paul refers to in this passage. What is obvious from this passage is that his needing to be harsh in confrontation left him with feelings of regret and turmoil.

We must understand that loving confrontation is not easy! It may leave you wondering if you have destroyed the relationship or if the confrontation is accomplishing anything positive. Fears and doubts may plague you even as they did the apostle Paul.

At the same time we must recognize the awesome potential of Spirit-led and loving confrontation. The Corinthians had responded with godly sorrow which led to repentance and restoration—these must be the goals of discerning love. By contrast, worldly sorrow, which does not involve repentance, leads to guilt and regret and ultimately to spiritual death. Too often worldly sorrow is sorrow at being caught rather than being sorry for sin.

6. According to 2 Corinthians 2:4-11, what emotions did Paul experience as he wrote the harsh letter?

What was his purpose?

What actions of love does he urge toward the sinning man at this point?

Why does he urge forgiveness (vv. 7,8,11)?

Do you feel the man had repented of his immorality? Why or why not?

Although these verses do not specifically say that the man had repented, it is highly unlikely that Paul would have encouraged the church to forgive and to receive him without an obvious change in behavior. It appears the church had taken the bold disciplinary actions that Paul had recommended and this individual had then responded in repentance. Following repentance, discerning love needed to reach out with forgiveness to restore that individual to fellowship where he could grow and mature in his Christian walk. *Repentance and restoration are always the goal of discerning love.*

A CALL TO THE MINISTRY OF RESTORATION

7. According to Galatians 6:1-3, what should we do when a fellow Christian falls into sin?

Describe what you think it means to "restore gently" (v. 1).

What caution should we take when seeking to restore another believer and why is this important?

What steps can one take to avoid falling into temptation while helping another individual overcome sin?

What are some practical ways that we can apply verse 2 when ministering to a believer who has fallen into sin?

Verse 2 states that carrying another's burdens will "fulfill the law of Christ." What does the "law of Christ" refer to? See John 13:34; Galatians 5:14 and James 2:8 for further clarification.

What attitude does verse 3 discourage and how will avoiding that attitude help us when we are seeking to restore another individual?

If you had been overtaken by sin, how would you want someone to act toward you?

When we see another believer who has been caught in the snare of sin, discerning love will act to help that individual overcome the sin and gain victory. Regrettably, Christians too often react in one or more of the following inappropriate ways:

- Ignoring the sin;
- Harshly attacking the sinner instead of the sin;
- Looking down on the individual;
- Gossiping about the person;
- Making no attempt to bring the individual to repentance and restoration.

In this passage, Paul urges the Galatians to be tender, yet firm—to forgive and help the sinner while confronting the sin. He urges them to be compassionate and not haughty in dealing with others. We must keep in mind that we are also prone to sin and we cannot think of ourselves as better than the one we are trying to help. Recognizing our own susceptibility to sin will help keep us gentle and humble as we seek to help others.

8. Read 2 Corinthians 10:12 and Galatians 6:4,5. What does verse 4 encourage each person to do for him- or herself?

How will testing your own actions help you as you seek to restore others?

What action is discouraged?

Why is comparing ourselves to others unwise?

What does verse 5 indicate regarding each person's responsibility?

Before we can really help another individual, it is important that we examine our own lives and test our own actions. We need to ask ourselves, *Are my actions godly and my motives pure?* If we cannot honestly say yes, then we need to ask God to purify our actions and our motives or we will not be able to restore others.

Comparisons are also detrimental in our efforts to help others. When we compare ourselves to others, the usual results are either feelings of inferiority or feelings of prideful superiority. Both of these attitudes are destructive and Paul prudently warns that those who "compare themselves with themselves...are not wise" (2 Corinthians 10:12).

When Paul urged the spiritually mature to help carry the "burdens" of others (v. 2), he was speaking of a load that is too heavy for one individual to carry. The Greek word for "burden" in verse 2 is different from the word used for "load" in verse 5. The word in verse 5 refers to a smaller load and implies a task or a service. Each individual should be encouraged to do his or her part; but when a person is facing a burden too heavy to carry, Christians need to lovingly step in to help carry that load, which may involve working to gently restore another believer who has slipped into sin.

9. According to 2 Timothy 2:25,26, how are God's servants encouraged to act toward those who oppose them?

What is the goal of gently instructing the opposing individual?

What do these verses imply about the manner in which genuine love confronts?

Discerning love is careful in the manner in which correction and confrontation are attempted. Bullying others into repentance seldom brings lasting results. Gentle instruction and the truth spoken in love (see Ephesians 4:15) are far more effective in achieving the desired repentance and restoration.

A Closer Look at My Own Heart

10. Read Philippians 1:8-11 from several different translations. How does the apostle Paul describe his love for the Philippians (v. 8)?

What did Paul's love lead him to do for the Philippians?

What did Paul pray for them in regard to their love (v. 9)?

The Greek word that is translated as "depth of insight" in the *New International Version* can also be properly translated as "discernment" in the *Modern Language Bible, New American Standard Bible, New King James Version* and *Revised Standard Version*.

What does it mean to you personally to have a love that *abounds* in knowledge and depth of insight or discernment?

Love without guidelines and boundaries is not a healthy love and is not the way God wants us to love. *Tolerating abuse, enabling addictions or condoning deliberate sin is not in the best interest of the other person.* As Paul prayed that the Philippians would "abound still more and more in real knowledge and all discernment" (Philippians 1:9, *NASB*), he identified two essential qualities of healthy love.

What is the result of love that abounds with knowledge and discernment?

As our love increases in knowledge and discernment, we will be able to recognize and approve what is best for our own lives and also in our actions toward others. Our lives will increasingly reflect Jesus' nature and He will be glorified.

11. Notice that Paul prays that their love will abound "more and more" in knowledge and discernment. This implies a growth process. Ask God to show you steps you can take to help your love grow in knowledge and discernment. Record the ideas that God reveals to you.

There will be times when we do not know how to best love another individual. Just as prayer was needed to help the Philippians grow in loving discernment, seeking God's guidance in prayer is essential to knowing how to love with a healthy love. Studying and knowing God's Word is another key to growing in wisdom and discernment. Sometimes we may also need to seek the objective advice of a godly counselor who can help us recognize unhealthy patterns and lead us to grow in discerning love.

12. According to James 1:5, what do we need to do when we lack wisdom?

What is promised to those who ask in faith for God's wisdom?

How does this promise apply to you and the areas where you need discernment in your love?

Action Steps I Can Take Today

13. **In what ways have you shown love in the past week?** In your journal, list the different ways you have shown love to others. Then evaluate those actions in regard to knowledge and discernment. Honestly answer the following questions:

    - Have my actions helped the other individual grow?
    - Have my actions in any way hindered God's work in his or her life?
    - Have I done for others what they needed to do for themselves?
    - Have my actions enabled others to continue in sin or in irresponsible behavior?
    - Have I spoken the truth in love?
    - Have my actions eliminated consequences that might have brought repentance?
    - Have my actions been aimed at trying to bring restoration?

14. **Ask God to show you any areas in which your actions of love may be enabling another individual to continue in sin;** then record in your journal the insights God reveals to you.

15. **Ask God to reveal where your love needs to grow in knowledge and to be more discerning.** Then ask God for a plan to help you grow in knowledge and discernment. Remember, God promises wisdom to those who ask for it (see James 1:5). In your journal, record the areas of needed growth along with the plan God gives to help you grow.

16. **Pray Philippians 1:9-11 daily.** On a 3x5-inch index card, write a paraphrase of Paul's prayer for the Philippians, personalizing it and making it a prayer to God for yourself. Keep the card in your Bible and pray this prayer every day this week and whenever you feel a need for greater discernment in your love.

- Eight -

LOVE COVERS OVER WRONGS AND IS PATIENT

Nothing in Sandi wanted her marriage to continue. She had been hurt too many times and as she reflected on past emotional wounds, she lost all hope of ever having a healthy marriage. Focusing on her husband's faults, they grew in magnitude and importance. Feelings of love were gone and Sandi was ready to end the marriage and get on with her life. She had lost patience and hope and quite simply no longer cared.

A Closer Look at the Problem

While divorce rates soar to unprecedented levels, is there any hope for a marriage like the one described above? Some wonder if it is even possible to build enduring love into a relationship. When love has seemingly died, is there any way to revitalize the feelings that originally drew the individuals together?

As we study this concluding chapter, we will see that God loves us with a patient and enduring love that does not magnify our sin, but covers over it with the precious blood of Jesus. He is in the business of restoring lives, restoring relationships and restoring marriages. Yes, through Jesus there *is* hope for troubled relationships. Love can be rekindled and revitalized, and sick relationships can be brought to health. The threefold focus of this chapter is to...

- See how God loves us with an enduring love that covers over our sin.
- Understand how love covers over wrongs.
- Learn how to build enduring love and renewed hope into relationships.

Before you begin your study, ask God to help you discern areas where your love needs to cover over wrongs; then give Him permission to change you. Will you ask Him to rekindle hope and love in relationships where you have been tempted to give up?

A Closer Look at God's Truth

1. Which phrase in 1 Peter 4:8 shows the importance of love?

   What action of love is described in this verse?

   Describe what you think is meant by the phrase "love covers over a multitude of sins."

   How and why do you think this happens?

In chapter 7, we learned that discerning love must sometimes confront sin in order to bring repentance and restoration. It is also important to recognize that discerning love is balanced and knows when to confront and when to overlook an offense. Every individual has weaknesses and we all sin. Hatred causes us to see every flaw, expose and magnify weaknesses and be quick to gossip and complain. By contrast, love helps us overlook minor flaws and weaknesses, seek to protect and not to draw attention to the character flaws of the loved individual.

2.   According to 2 Corinthians 5:14-21, for whom did Christ die?

What else has God, through Christ, done for us (vv. 18,19)?

What did Christ become for us and what is the result for us (v. 21)?

How do these verses demonstrate Jesus' love that covers over our sin?

What does the phrase "we might become the righteousness of God" (v. 21) mean to you?

3.   Which phrases in Isaiah 61:10 indicate God's love covers over sin?

When Jesus died on the cross, He paid the penalty for our sin by becoming sin for us, and in exchange He gave us His righteousness. When God looks at a believer, He looks at that individual through the blood of Jesus and He sees that believer as righteous. Through the sacrifice of Jesus, God's love has covered over and forgiven our sin. Accepting His love and forgiveness toward us helps us to accept ourselves and enables us to reach out with His love toward others.

4.   What does it mean to you personally to be seen by God as righteous because of your faith in Jesus? Take a few minutes to ponder this blessing; then write a prayer of thanksgiving for His great love that covers over your sin.

If you have never accepted Jesus as your Savior and Lord, will you choose to invite Him into your heart and life today? His love is eager and willing to cover the sin in your life and to give you His righteousness. If you desire to receive Jesus, simply acknowledge that you are a sinner and ask Him to forgive you. Invite Him to come into your life and take control. He will graciously forgive and cover over your sin and you will receive His righteousness. If you take this vital step, it is important that you share what you have done with another believer who can encourage you and rejoice with you.

REACHING OUT WITH A LOVE THAT COVERS

The story of Noah and his three sons illustrates the difference between an action that exposes and love that covers over.

5. According to Genesis 9:18-27, how did Ham respond to seeing his father naked and drunk?

    How did Shem and Japheth respond?

    What was the result of Ham's actions (vv. 24,25)?

    How were Shem and Japheth rewarded (vv. 26,27)?

Even the righteous Noah had an obvious character flaw and Ham saw the results. At that point, Ham had the choice of either covering his father or further exposing him. He chose to tell his brothers about their father's shameful condition. By contrast, Shem and Japheth chose to not look, but rather to cover over their father's nakedness.

When we become aware of the character flaws of those around us, we also have choices. We can gossip and further expose the individual or we can cover that person with love and prayers while seeking to help him or her overcome the character flaws.

It is important to note that Shem and Japheth were blessed because of their act of kindness while Ham was cursed because of his actions. When we seek to expose another, we lose blessings and invite curses in the process.

6. What do the following verses reveal about love, gossip and malicious words?

Proverbs 10:12

Proverbs 16:28

Proverbs 17:9

Proverbs 26:20-22

What does it show when you gossip about another?

How is gossip the opposite of a love that covers over?

What are some ways we can demonstrate a love that covers over sin?

In marked contrast to a love that covers over sin is gossip that delights in *uncovering* and *exposing* the faults of others. The person who loves does not want to draw attention to the faults and shortcomings of the one he or she loves. While it may sometimes be necessary to expose and confront sin in order to bring restoration to the other individual, it is never done with pleasure nor with the purpose of hurting the individual and his or her reputation. *Love always seeks to help—never to hurt.*

7. In Titus 3:1-3, what instructions regarding our speech are found in verse 2?

How is the unbeliever described (v. 3)?

8. In Titus 3:4-11, what attributes of God are given in verses 4 and 5?

What actions in verses 4 through 7 demonstrate the love of God that covers over sin?

Why did God do these things for us?

What should believers be careful to do and why (v. 8)?

What should be avoided and why?

What does verse 11 tell about a person who causes division?

How do gossip and foolish arguments contribute to divisions within a church or family?

What can we do to prevent gossip and foolish arguments?

If we are going to love as Jesus loves, we must refuse to allow ourselves to become part of gossip sessions. This means we will not gossip ourselves and we will not participate as listeners. The tales we hear go into our innermost being and become a part of the way we think of others. The more we gossip and complain about a person's faults, the worse they will appear to become. Although it may be necessary to confront an individual regarding sin in his or her life, exposing the faults of another through gossip is *never* a loving action. Ask God to give you discernment to recognize when it is in the best interest of another individual to cover over his or her sin and when confrontation is necessary. Before taking action, ask yourself, *What is truly in the best interest of the other individual?*

9.   In Psalm 32:1-5, how does David describe the individual whose sins are covered (vv. 1,2)?

How do these verses demonstrate the difference between love that *covers over* sin (vv. 1,2) and the attempt to *cover up* sin (vv. 3-5)?

How does David contrast the emotional effects of love that covers over sin with his attempt to cover up sin?

It is important to recognize that love which covers over sin is not the same as an unhealthy attempt to *cover up* sin. In Psalm 32, David describes the intense agony that he felt while trying to cover up his adultery with Bathsheba and the murder of her husband, Uriah (see 2 Samuel 11—12). The purpose of the cover-up was to deceive, and God was displeased. In love, God sent the prophet Nathan to confront David.

Love that covers over sin, recognizes and acknowledges the sin, yet continues to love while seeking to bring healing and restoration. Discerning love addresses the sin and will confront when needed, but seeks to help the loved one overcome the sin. *Love that covers over can love the sinner without condoning the sin.* It looks at the sinner's shortcomings through love that covers over the sin with the healing balm of mercy and forgiveness, always seeking restoration. Covering up or denying abuse, deliberate sin or addictive behavior will not bring the healing and restoration we desire and should not be confused with love that covers over sin with mercy and forgiveness (see chapter 7 for further study of discerning love). In contrast to the healing potential of love that covers over sin, covering up deliberate sin is like applying a bandage to a dirty wound. Instead of healing, the wound is likely to become infected and create long-term problems.

10.   Which phrases in 1 Corinthians 13:4-7 relate to gossip or love that covers over wrong?

Which phrases speak of patience as an action of love?

11.   According to James 5:7-11, how long are we encouraged to be patient?

What three examples of patience are given in this passage?

How does this passage define patience?

How is a farmer an example of patience?

How are Job and the prophets examples of patience?

What is encouraged in verse 8 and why?

What action contrary to patience are we to avoid and why?

Why were the prophets regarded as happy or "blessed" (v. 11)?

12.   In Job 42:10-17, how did God reward Job's patience?

We often think that being patient means that we will never lose our tempers. While patience will often help us to control our anger, the passage from James 5 defines patience as endurance or perseverance. Remaining in a difficult marriage or in any other unfulfilling relationship is not easy. Many people are quick to leave a marriage that they find does not meet their needs, and it seems easier to leave a church or dissolve a friendship than it is to work on correcting problems. While God does not expect us to live in dangerous and abusive situations, His kind of love does not easily give up. Agape love that always seeks the highest good for the other individual will seek a resolution to the difficulties whenever possible.

A Closer Look at My Own Heart

There are times when discouragement threatens to overwhelm and the desire to give up on a relationship can be very strong. The remaining Scripture passages of this chapter contain promises that can help bring us hope when we are struggling with discouragement. As you study these promises, apply them to your own situation. Remember that God's love for you is a love that does not give up, and He will help you build that same kind of love into your life if you sincerely seek His help.

13. Read the following verses and personalize the promises found in each, applying them to your own relationships:

Proverbs 16:7

Proverbs 21:21

Hebrews 4:14-16

Which promise from these verses is most meaningful to you and why? Memorize and personalize that promise. Write it on an index card and place it where you will see it often and be reminded that this is God's promise to you.

14. As you read Galatians 6:7-10, list the warnings found in verse 7.

What spiritual truths illustrated by nature are expressed in verses 7 and 8?

How can these truths be a warning?

How can they be a promise?

How can verses 7 and 8 relate to loving others?

Ask God to show you "seeds," or actions, of love that you can sow into the life of another. List the actions that God brings to your mind.

What does verse 9 urge us to avoid?

What promise is given?

What is the condition for reaping the harvest?

What does verse 10 encourage us to do?

The principle of sowing and reaping illustrates several spiritual truths that can be applied to loving others.

1. **We will reap what we sow.** If we sow seeds of love, love will grow in our own lives and our relationships will become more loving. If we sow seeds of bitterness, discord or resentment, we can only expect the same in return.

2. **We will reap in proportion to the amount that we sow.** If we are stingy in the actions of love we give out, the love that comes back to us will be small. If we choose to love abundantly and freely, our harvest of love will be ample.

3. **Seeds that are planted need time to grow.** They must be watered and nurtured until they produce a harvest. To quit watering during a dry spell would greatly reduce the possibility of a good harvest. If our loving actions do not produce immediate results, we are often tempted to give up. If we want results, we must give the seeds time to grow.

In these verses, the apostle Paul urged the Galatians to refuse to give up and to keep sowing the good seeds that will bring forth a godly harvest. Let us also determine to keep sowing seeds of love. Claim God's promise that you will reap a harvest if you do not give up. With God's help, we can continue to nurture those seeds of love until they bring forth a harvest of love.

15. What is requested in the prayer of 1 Thessalonians 3:12,13?

What would be the result?

Action Steps I Can Take Today

16. **Paraphrase the words of 1 Thessalonians 3:12,13 into your own personal prayer to God.** Record this prayer in your journal and on a 3x5-inch index card. Place it where you will see it often and be reminded to pray it regularly.

17. **Evaluate your own life in regard to your willingness to cover over sin.** Ask God to make you aware of any areas in which you need to cover another's sin with mercy and forgiveness. Ask Him to help you discern between godly love that covers over sin and unhealthy love that seeks to deceive by covering up deliberate sin and abusive actions. Record in your journal what God reveals to you.

18. **Evaluate your speech for gossip and tearing down others.** Ask God to reveal to you any areas where you may be falling into gossip or using words to tear down others. Gossip can be carefully disguised as "Christian concern" or "prayer requests." If we are not a part of the problem or a part of the solution, we should not encourage gossip by listening. Record in your journal what God reveals to you.

19. **Carefully monitor what comes out of your mouth.** Before speaking, ask yourself the following:

    - Is what I am saying true?
    - Is it necessary?
    - Is it kind?
    - Will it build up or tear down?

20. **Evaluate your level of love by reviewing the different actions of love** you've studied in this book. Ask God to show you which actions of love are most needed in your own life. Will you ask God's help in devising a plan to add those actions to your life? Record in your journal the plan of action that God reveals to you. Share with another believer what God is revealing and ask that individual to help you by praying for and with you and by checking your progress in the future.

21. **Do not hesitate to seek help from a godly Christian counselor** if you need further help in building love into your life. Sometimes we need the help of a godly professional trained in biblical counseling to help us overcome some of the stumbling blocks to love. The sooner you get help, the quicker you will begin to grow.

22. **Allow God's love to empower you to love others.** Never forget that God loves and values you immensely. He is always available to help you learn to walk in love and victory. As you seek His face and draw into His presence, His love in you will enable you to love others.

May the Lord make your love increase and overflow for each other and for everyone else, just as ours does for you. May he strengthen your hearts so that you will be blameless and holy in the presence of our God and Father when our Lord Jesus comes with all his holy ones (1 Thessalonians 3:12,13).

What Is Aglow International?

——⁂——

From one nation to 135 worldwide...
From one fellowship to over 3,300...
From 100 women to more than 2 million...

Aglow International has experienced phenomenal growth since its inception 30 years ago. In 1967, four women from the state of Washington prayed for a way to reach out to other Christian women in simple fellowship, free from denominational boundaries.

——⁂——

The first meeting held in Seattle, Washington, USA, drew more than 100 women to a local hotel. From that modest beginning, Aglow International has become one of the largest intercultural, interdenominational women's organizations in the world.

——⁂——

Each month, Aglow touches the lives of an estimated two million women on six continents through local fellowship meetings, Bible studies, support groups, retreats, conferences and various outreaches. From the inner city to the upper echelons, from the woman next door to the corporate executive, Aglow seeks to minister to the felt needs of women around the world.

——⁂——

Christian women find Aglow a "safe place" to grow spiritually and begin to discover and use the gifts, talents and abilities God has given them. Aglow offers excellent leadership training and varied opportunities to develop those leadership skills.

——⁂——

Undergirding the evangelistic thrust of the ministry is an emphasis on prayer, which has led to an active prayer network linking six continents. The vast prayer power available through Aglow women around the world is being used by God to influence countless lives in families, communities, cities and nations.

Aglow's Mission Statement

Our mission is to lead women to Jesus Christ and
provide opportunity for Christian women to grow in
their faith and minister to others.

———∞———

Aglow's Continuing Focus...

- To reconcile woman to her womanhood as God
  designed. To strengthen and empower her to fulfill the
  unfolding plan of God as He brings restoration to the
  male/female relationship, which is the foundation of
  the home, the church and the community.
- To love women of all cultures with a special focus on
  Muslim women.
- To reach out to every strata of society, from inner
  cities to isolated outposts to our own neighborhoods,
  with very practical and tangible expressions of the
  love of Jesus.

———∞———

Gospel Light and Aglow International present an important
new series of Bible studies for use in small groups.
Look for other studies in the Aglow Bible Study Series:
**Shame: Thief of Intimacy, Keys to Contentment, Fashioned for
Intimacy Study Guide**, companion to the book **Fashioned for
Intimacy, Building Better Relationships, God's Character,
Walk Out of Worry, A Woman After God's Heart** and
Forgiveness at your local bookstore,
or contact Gospel Light.
For information about these and other outstanding Bible study
resources from Aglow, call us at 1-800-793-8126.

Aglow Ministers In...

Albania, Angola, Anguilla, Antigua, Argentina, Aruba, Australia, Austria, Bahamas, Bahrain, Barbados, Belarus, Belgium, Belize, Benin, Bermuda, Bolivia, Botswana, Brazil, Britain, Bulgaria, Burkina Faso, Cameroon, Canada, Chile, China, Colombia, Congo (Dem. Rep. of), Congo (Rep. of), Costa Rica, Côte d'Ivoire, Cuba, Curaçao, Czech Republic, Denmark, Djibouti, Dominica, Dominican Republic, Ecuador, Egypt, El Salvador, Equatorial Guinea, Estonia, Ethiopia, Faroe Islands, Fiji, Finland, France, Gabon, the Gambia, Germany, Ghana, Grand Cayman, Greece, Grenada, Guam, Guatemala, Guinea, Guyana, Haiti, Honduras, Hungary, Iceland, India, Indonesia, Ireland, Israel, Jamaica, Japan, Kazakstan, Kenya, Korea, Kyrgyzstan, Latvia, Lithuania, Malawi, Malaysia, Mali, Mauritius, Mexico, Mongolia, Mozambique, Myanmar, Nepal, Netherlands, New Zealand, Nicaragua, Niger, Nigeria, Norway, Oman, Pakistan, Panama, Papua New Guinea, Peru, Philippines, Portugal, Puerto Rico, Romania, Russia, Rwanda, Samoa, Samoa (American), Scotland, Senegal, Serbia, Sierra Leone, Singapore, South Africa, Spain, Sri Lanka, St. Kitts, St. Lucia, St. Maartan, St. Vincent, Sudan, Suriname, Sweden, Switzerland, Tajikistan, Tanzania, Thailand, Togo, Tonga, Trinidad/Tobago, Turks & Caicos Islands, Uganda, Ukraine, United States, Uruguay, Uzbekistan, Venezuela, Vietnam, Virgin Islands (American), Virgin Islands (British), Wales, Yugoslavia, Zambia, Zimbabwe, plus one extremely restricted 10/40 Window nation.

How do I find my nearest Aglow Fellowship? Call or write us at:

AGLOW
INTERNATIONAL

P.O. Box 1749, Edmonds, WA 98020-1749
Phone: 425-775-7282 or 1-800-793-8126
Fax: 1-800-860-3109   E-mail: aglow@aglow.org
Web site: http://www.aglow.org/

The Aglow Bible Study Series

Walk Out of Worry
Choosing God's Path
to Peace
Janice Wise
Trade Paper
ISBN 08307.24141
$6.99

Forgiveness
Learning to Be
Forgiven and to
Forgive from the Heart
Eva Gibson
Trade Paper
ISBN 08307.24184
$6.99

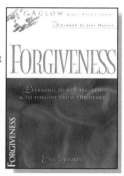

A Woman After God's Heart
Discovering Your Legacy
as God's Daughter
Eadie Goodboy
Trade Paper
ISBN 08307.24133
$6.99

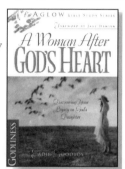

Loving As Jesus Loves
Sharon A. Steele
Trade Paper
ISBN 08307.25040
$6.99

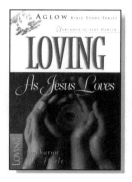

Building Better Relationships
How to Put Love into Action
Bobbie Yagel
Trade Paper
ISBN 08307.21320 $6.99

Choosing to Change
How to Aquire the Mind of Christ
Sharon A. Steele
Trade Paper
ISBN 08307.21312 $6.99

Shame: Thief of Intimacy
Unmasking the Accuser
Marie Powers
Trade Paper
ISBN 08307.21290 $6.99

God's Character
A Study of His Attributes
*Eadie Goodboy
and Agnes Lawless*
Trade Paper
ISBN 08307.23226 $6.99

Keys to Contentment
Sharon A. Steele
Trade Paper
ISBN 08307.21304 $6.99

Fashioned for Intimacy
*Jane Hansen
and Marie Powers*
Trade Paper
ISBN 08307.23128 $6.99
Video
UPC 607135.003649 $39.99

Available at your local Christian bookstore.

Gospel Light